ALL

MOTHERS

WORK

ALL MOTHERS WORK

CINDY RAMMING

AVON BOOKS ◆ NEW YORK

VISIT OUR WEBSITE AT
http://AvonBooks.com

ALL MOTHERS WORK is an original publication of Avon Books. This work has
never before appeared in book form.

AVON BOOKS
A division of
The Hearst Corporation
1350 Avenue of the Americas
New York, New York 10019

Library of Congress Cataloging in Publication Data:

Ramming, Cindy.
  All mothers work / by Cindy Ramming.
     p.   cm.
1. Working mothers. 2. Mothers. 3. Work and family. I. Title.
HQ759.48.R37 1996   96-19394
306.874'3—dc20   CIP

First Avon Books Trade Printing: December 1996

AVON TRADEMARK REG. U.S. PAT. OFF. AND IN OTHER COUNTRIES, MARCA REGISTRADA, HECHO
EN U.S.A.

Printed in the U.S.A.

OPM   10 9 8 7 6 5 4 3 2 1

To
Kristl Volk Franklin

(She loves to see her name in print.)

ACKNOWLEDGMENTS

Writing tends to be a solitary journey, but fortunately, this author enjoyed the company of many other travelers along the road. Some served as sources of inspiration, keeping me going when the going got tough; others offered me shelter and rest along the way; and a few helped keep me focused on the final destination.

So, thanks to all of you who traveled with me to the completion of this book. To the members of my critique group, Kristl Franklin, Catherine Duerr, Cindy Garbett, Tammi Easterday, Beverly Peek, Michael Pipkin, and Cindy Vincent, thanks for saying, "I like it, but . . ."

Thanks to my family, especially my husband, Arnold, and our son, Ryan, for putting up with the late night writing sessions and missed appointments—*and* for constantly reminding me why I wanted to write this book in the first place. To my mom and dad, June and Win Laughlin, who raised me to believe that I could do anything—thanks for your wisdom (and the great quotes).

Finally, heartfelt thanks to the Friend of all the weary, who opens windows when doors close, and offers hope to all the children of the world, even us moms and dads.

I take great comfort in believing that we are not alone.

CONTENTS

Contents

PREFACE

Motherhood. The final frontier. These are the stories of mothers everywhere. Our ongoing mission: to seek out a more meaningful life, to help create a better civilization, to boldly go where no mother has gone before.

The stories you are about to read are true. (Well, some of them are. All of them are true in spirit.) The names have *not* been changed, although the author did limit identification to first names only, having resisted the strong temptation to parenthetically add: You know who you are!

Your mission, should you decide to accept it, is to embark upon a journey into a new dimension of time and space. Your destination: The Working Mother Zone.

LET'S GET
ONE THING STRAIGHT

All mothers work. Oh, maybe a few of us are in a coma or something, but by and large, we all work. So the next time you ask a mother, "Do you work?" just save us all some time and give yourself a swift kick in the sit-down and move on to more intelligent conversation.

Now, of course, I know when we ask "that question" (and I admit to having asked it myself), what we really *mean* is, "Do you work *outside the home?*" What we really want to *know* is, "Do we have anything in common?" or "Is this someone who could join my car pool?" But what we *say* is, "Do you work?"

Allow me to repeat myself. Some mothers have a second job through which they earn money. But all mothers work.

Now that that's settled, we're free to examine some of the

more pressing questions mothers face these days: How do we choose the work that's best for our own well-being and the well-being of our families? If we're financially able, how do we choose between staying home and getting a job? How are we going to get our kids to adulthood without losing them to drugs or violence? How did Oprah really lose all that weight?

Well, we can't answer every question in the scope of one book, so we're going to focus on work—specifically, the working choices mothers face. We're going to take an honest look at those choices and maybe even discover some choices we didn't know we had. We're going to try to make the best of where we are, and where we want to be.

I can't claim to be "every woman" (unlike Oprah). What I am is the mother of a ten-year-old son. I have a husband who has a job. I have alternately been a stay-at-home mom and a "working" mom (office manager, accountant, business manager, corporate officer), with gusts of in-home businesses such as selling makeup and educational toys. Like you, I deal with issues of money, day care, money, "quality time," piano lessons, money, Little League, money, school, laundry, homework, money, scouts, and my favorite recurring nightmare: "What's for supper?" Oh, yes, and there's also money. Having worked both in and out of the home, I hope to shed some light on this very confusing issue, and dispel a few myths along the way.

But this book is not for everyone. It is for you who have a *choice* to work in or out of the home. It is for you who are struggling with working outside the home and wondering if you have choices that you didn't know about. It is for you who have been forced out of the workplace because your job doesn't exist anymore. It is for you who have chosen to stay home and are tired of being asked, "Do you work?" It is for all of us who wish there was a better way.

I'd like to help you sort it all out.

So let's get to work!

PART ONE

❧

Is "Working" Working?

It's a jungle out there.
—Tarzan

CHAPTER 1 ∽

DOLLARS AND SENSE

(WARNING: If you are currently employed, reading this chapter may be hazardous to your mental health.)

Beware of all enterprises that require new clothes.
— HENRY DAVID THOREAU, 1849

"IF YOU'VE GOT THE MONEY, HONEY . . ."

Why do mothers work outside the home in the first place? I hear a resounding chorus of "Money!" ringing in response. Some are humming a nice little "self-fulfillment" countermelody, but most of us are singing along with the "cash chorus."

We need money to live. Each of us exists in a lifestyle that requires a certain amount of money to maintain. For some, the requirements are food and shelter. Others may "need" food, shelter, cable TV, and a country club membership. Whatever your list includes, as soon as you get a job outside the home, add these to it: child care, transportation, eating out, wardrobe, and additional taxes—to name but a few of the things that will separate you from your money.

You see, many of us operate under the mistaken assumption that just because we're getting a paycheck every couple of

5

weeks or so, we're making money. 'Tain't necessarily so! We do get to deposit a check into our bank account—or to cash it. That part is fun. What isn't fun is having to turn around and spend much of our hard-earned money paying for things that make it possible for us to work in the first place!

What really isn't fun is what I'm possibly about to do to you: burst your paycheck bubble. I call it, "Don't laugh all the way to the bank just yet!" This is one of those times in your life that you can't get past unless you go through it (like childbirth). But don't worry, we'll go through together.

Let me tell you a little story.

Oh, Joy!

Joy rubbed her eyes when the evening rush-hour traffic stopped for a moment. She took a deep breath, trying to shake off the exhaustion of the day. Securely buckled into his car seat, eleven-month-old Herby sat behind her. *At least he's quiet today*, she thought, grateful for the silence.

Honk! The car behind her notified Joy that the light had changed.

"Give it a rest," she muttered under her breath, then glanced at the dashboard clock as her foot pressed the accelerator. Automatically she checked the rearview mirror, and groaned slightly when she saw that Herby had fallen asleep.

Now he'll be up all night, she thought, *and I've got that report due at 10 A.M. tomorrow! I've got to get some sleep tonight!* She mentally checked off all the things left to do for the report—too many to complete if she waited until 8 A.M. to arrive at work. She had to get there early! How could she get the rest she needed if Herby was off schedule?

Maybe Dan would do the midnight duty tonight, she thought, and then sighed. Dan would be happy to try, but she knew Herby, and when Herby stayed up late, the whole family stayed up with him.

Joy glanced at the clock again. The LCD indicated that only two minutes had passed since she last checked.

I live my life by minutes, she thought. *Twenty-two minutes to Herby's day care. Eleven minutes to sign him out and get his things. Seven minutes to put him in the car. Twenty-eight minutes to get home.* She stopped herself, refusing to continue the litany of her minute-by-minute existence. Turning on the radio, she tried to concentrate on the music, but her mind pulled back to all the things she had to accomplish this evening. And, not for the first time, she wondered where she was going to find the energy to get it all done.

"If we didn't need the money . . ." she said out loud, but wouldn't allow herself to complete the thought. She remembered how, twelve minutes ago, the baby's day care provider told her that little Herby had taken his first tentative step today. "Miss Sarah" had beamed with pride as she shared this news with Joy, who had struggled to hold back unexpected tears . . .

Later, after supper and four-year-old Hannah's bath and bedtime story, Joy sat down to rock Herby, his head resting on her shoulder as he snuggled against her. As Dan finished cleaning the kitchen, Joy looked hopefully at the clock over the fireplace: 8:30 P.M. If she could get Herby down by 9, she still had a chance to get that much-needed sleep.

Just then Herby arched back and gave her one of his captivating, heart-stopping grins. Then he squirmed, letting her know he wanted down. Knowing it was pointless to restrain him, she placed him on the floor, then watched him crawl over to his toy basket by the fireplace. He reached up and pulled the basket over, giggling with delight as the toys scattered noisily on the floor.

Joy dropped her head into her hands. "I'm not going to get any sleep tonight!"

Joy is in a dilemma. She would rather stay home with her two children, but feels she must work to contribute to the family financially. A responsible woman who wants the best for her family, she's doing the best she can. She's put a lot of energy into her career as a bookkeeper, and makes a good salary of $25,000 per year.

According to 1993 Department of Labor statistics, the median salary of the nation's workers (all genders) is $24,076 annually.

Women earn roughly 77 cents for every dollar a man earns.

The median income for college educated women is $25,818. However, "About 80% of women workers earn less than $25,000 a year. Only 400,000 women workers in the U.S.—out of 58 million—earn more than $75,000 a year." (*Working Mother* Magazine, May 1994, "The Challenge Ahead," by Karen Nussbaum.)

Her two children, Hannah and Herby, are in separate day cares—one for babies and one for older children. Hannah's care costs Joy $15 per day, while the baby's is $25 per day. It's all Joy can do to get the kids ready in the morning, so she chooses to eat lunch out every day, which costs her about $5 a day. The family eats dinner out every Friday (Joy's little reward to herself for getting through another week), and they spend between $25 and $40 on that. She and Dan agreed that having a maid come in twice a month would free up some of their family time, and that costs them $50 every other week.

Let's see if working works for Joy:

Salary per eight-hour day ($12/hour)	$96.00
Less: work-related expenses	
Income Tax (28%)	-27.00
Social Security Tax	-8.00

Childcare Expense	-40.00
Extra Daily Gasoline Expense	-2.00
Lunch Out	-5.00
Maid (pro-rated per day expense)	-5.00
Eating out with family (pro-rated)	-5.00
Net Pay Per Day	$ 4.00
Net Pay Per Hour	50 cents !!!

Wow! Working outside the home *costs* Joy $92 a day! If she knew that, I wonder if she would make some different choices in her life.

According to the U.S. Census Bureau, families spend an estimated $21.8 billion on child care each year. Each family spends an *average* of $3,600 per year, per child. In some parts of the country, high-quality infant care can cost as much as $1,100 *per month*!

We've looked at Joy's expenses, and maybe you're wondering why so much is taken out for taxes? The sad fact that Joy (and all working wives) must face is this: The IRS is going to get theirs. If you are considering staying home, you have to examine how much money you pay out in taxes when you and your husband are both working, and how much you would pay out if one of you stays home.

Whoa! Do I hear some groans? You're not alone. Many people balk at the mere mention of taxes and the IRS. That's why H&R Block does such a good business. But trust me, unless you have a very complicated tax situation, it's not too difficult to figure out the additional taxes you pay *as a couple* when both of you work versus the taxes you pay when only one of you works. And if you do have a very complicated tax situation, chances are you have a CPA who can figure it out for you.

Essentially, the way it works for most of us is that the second wage earner, in this case the wife, starts paying taxes at the rate where the first wage earner left off.

In Joy's case, her husband's income, after it has been adjusted for all the deductions to which the family is entitled, puts the couple in the 28 percent tax bracket. That means that every additional dollar that comes into the household (i.e., Joy's salary) is taxed at the rate of 28 percent, at least until they reach the next tax bracket.

During one of our better financial years, when I had a corporate officer job, we were paying federal taxes at the highest level at that time: 33 percent. We also live in California, which means we had to pay state income taxes (Oh, Joy!—pun intended) at the rate of 10 percent. The state also charges a couple of other cute little taxes. Let's not forget the mandatory Social Security and Medicare taxes, which at that time was a combined 7.65 percent. So, let's see. That means that my terrific (and it really was) professional salary was being taxed, every pay period, to the tune of 33 percent plus 10 percent plus 1.2 percent (those cute little state taxes) plus 7.65 percent. That means I was paying 51.85 percent of my salary—*over half*—in taxes.

Oh, goody. Out of the 48.15 percent of my salary that I actually got to keep, I then had the privilege of spending $300 each month on day care, buying lunch out every day, taking the family out to dinner (in our case) three to five times each week, buying more gasoline to drive all over town every day getting to day care and then work, etcetera, ad nauseam. I also "had" to buy an expensive wardrobe of quality clothing for the office (but I won't tell you I didn't enjoy that part).

In the interest of fairness and before we go any further I need to point out that I was also entitled to receive a tax credit for dependent care expenses. This tax credit is one way the IRS tries to lessen the impact of that whopping tax rate the second family wage earner is required to pay. The credit varies widely based on a variety of factors, but when I was working the maximum credit available to me was $960 per year.

Joy is entitled to this credit as well, but I didn't include it in her daily wage and expense calculation. On the other hand,

I also didn't include her wardrobe expense, which would offset the credit. Add to that the fact that there are probably a myriad of other little things Joy spends money on because she's working that I didn't even list. For the purposes of this illustration, let's just agree that the benefit of Joy's child care tax credit is eaten up by miscellaneous other work-related expenses.

And speaking of other expenses, if Joy lived in California (one of thirty-nine states that have some sort of state income tax), she'd be paying out an additional $6 to $8 per day in state taxes. We figured out that she was making $4 each day after all her expenses. The last time I checked, $4 minus $8 was not a positive number. That's *scary*!

Now, some of you may be thinking things like: *What if her husband doesn't work? What if she's a single mother?* I respectfully refer you back to the introductory section ("Let's Get One Thing Straight"), paragraph seven. If you're not inclined to turn the pages I'll repeat myself: This book is not for everyone! (I read somewhere that people have to hear something seven times before they remember it. That's two.)

Our friend Joy is working because her family "needs the money." For the moment we'll assume that she doesn't have to pay state income taxes and she is bringing home that lovely $4 a day, or roughly $86 per month, a far cry from the $2,083 per month at the top of her paycheck. It is possible that Joy and Dan's budget is so tight that they absolutely have to have that additional $86. That $86 might be paying the electric bill, or part of a car payment.

It is also possible that a portion of that money goes toward expenses that Joy and Dan could omit from their family budget without reducing their lifestyle—things like cable television, professional manicures, and eating out a lot.

The real question is, what choices would Joy make if she knew that her $25,000 annual salary was really bringing her only $86 extra each month? At the very least, I think she would reevaluate her situation. She would have to decide if that $86 was worth what it was costing her. And she'd better hope that

ONE MOM PUTS IN HER TWO CENTS WORTH

Cheri, a twenty-eight-year-old mom in Southern California, recently took an honest look at her working situation. A language arts teacher in English and reading, she began to question just how much her job was costing her:

"Until I sat down and did the calculations, I thought it really *was* better (financially, that is!) for me to work outside the home. I was dumbfounded to find out how *little* I get to keep! And it's true—because I have an outside job, I feel like I deserve to/can afford to buy little extras that really eat up what little I actually bring home. [After paying for child care] . . . I'd keep only $300–$400 a month, and a lot of that would go to pay for ready-made clothes for me and the kids, convenience foods, gas, etc.!"

she doesn't have another baby—she can't afford another day care bill!

IT'S LIKE MONEY IN THE BANK

I once worked for a company that thought we employees weren't appreciative enough of our paychecks. To educate and inform us (and maybe to induce a little guilt as well), it decided to show us how much it paid us over and above our paychecks.

Huh? Are we talking about a box of candy at Christmas? No, we're talking about benefits, a major reason many of us choose to work outside the home. We're talking health insurance, paid vacations and holidays, pension plan, profit sharing, subsidized and/or on-site child care, life insurance, sick leave, and the like. The company I worked for sent us each a list of the things we got that they paid for, and that list was quite an eye-opener.

In Joy's case, if her employer provides health insurance at no cost to her, but it costs them $1,200 a year to insure her, in a sense she's making an additional $1,200 a year. I'm assuming that Joy would buy health insurance for herself if she wasn't employed. I'm also assuming that Joy *could* buy health insurance for herself at the same rate her employer pays. (The reality is that individuals generally pay more for health insurance than employers do for insuring large groups of people.)

It's possible that you work for an employer that not only pays for your health coverage, but also pays for all or a part of your family's health coverage as well. Wow! Where do we sign up? This is a great benefit!

Each employer's benefits are different. One rule of thumb is that the bigger the company, the better the benefits. You may even belong to a union that negotiates benefits for you. Smaller companies may have fewer benefits (such as fewer paid holidays), but they may also be more flexible in granting time off, which could be considered an intangible benefit to moms like us. Flexible time off is especially important to a mother whose kids may actually get sick on occasion.

Some of these benefits, such as retirement plans or sick pay, will be hard to calculate to the penny. I suggest you just make a list of the benefits you have at your job (if any), and keep those in mind as you look at your options. Think about what it would cost you to replace those benefits, such as health insurance, if you decided to leave your job. If Joy has kids with major medical problems, working for a net 50 cents an hour may be worth it for her. Every situation is different.

Money talks

There's always a catch. Calculating how much your job costs you is a place to start, but it's not the end of the story. There are some other aspects to this money thing that you need to look at if you're going to evaluate what you're getting out of working against what working is costing you.

You see, there's more to money than meets the eye, or even the checkbook. Sure, most of us go to work to put food on the table, but we also get a big emotional paycheck, wouldn't you agree? That money in your pocket on payday, whether you've already spent it on daycare and taxes or not, can make you feel pretty darn good about yourself. It's like carrying a little sign around in your pocket that says, "I'm valuable. I'm worth something. And I have the paycheck to prove it."

Money—specifically what feels like *your own money*—can help you feel more independent. In my own case, I really (and I mean, *really*) enjoyed shopping for those new clothes. I needed the clothes, after all, for my job. And fortunately, my job provided the funds I needed to pay for the clothes I needed for my job. Each payday I'd look at that wonderful little piece of paper with my name on it, followed by a dollar sign and some numbers. That was *my* name on the check—no one else's. The check almost spoke to me: "Spend me, I'm yours. You worked hard for me. You deserve it. You *need* clothes."

I couldn't wait to get to the bank and deposit that little booger into our checking account. Because we'd operated on a bare-bones budget for years, seeing how my paycheck made that account balance go up made me feel as if we had all kinds of money, extra money—*my money*. I felt so fortunate that the bank was on the way to the mall—and my favorite clothing store. And what a rush I got out of writing that check for my new clothes! I can tell you, the employees of that store smiled when they saw me coming.

Money is a powerful motivator. When you're evaluating whether working works for you, take this into consideration. What kind of power does your paycheck give you? Do you, like me, enjoy the power of making a bee-line to the mall on payday? Maybe your power trip is depositing your paycheck into a growing savings account, or that feeling of satisfaction you get when you buy the weekly groceries, knowing you'll be able to pay for them without any problem. And how about that "my money" feeling—does it make you tingle? Money talks. What is it saying to you?

You probably want to keep these feelings in mind as you evaluate your choices. I never promised you this was going to be easy! I just want to help you sort out the issues in a way that helps you make the choices that are right for you.

IT ALL COMES DOWN TO CHOICES

You have the power to choose. You get *something* out of working, or you wouldn't do it. What does your job give you? How much is your job costing you? It is impossible to make a rational decision about your life without the facts and, trust me, the salary at the top of your pay stub is not a fact until you have adjusted it for those work-related expenses. Going through the calculation may change your perspective. Or it may reinforce your decision to stay in the workforce. Either way, aren't you better off knowing the truth? I'm not trying to tell you that you *have* to come home or that you *have* to work. You're smart enough to figure out your own life. I do want to encourage you to take a look at your options, and looking at the money part of it is a good place to start.

When I applied this little calculation process to my own job, I discovered that my terrific professional salary was reduced to about $3.50 an hour, after expenses, and taking into account my paid health insurance. This tidbit of information caused me to rethink why I was working outside the home in the first place. I was exhausted most of the time and under stress all the time. I could barely keep up with my own schedule, much less keep track of what was going on with my family.

Oh, sure. Work was fulfilling. It's fun being with grown-ups and solving problems and going out to lunch and getting a paycheck every two weeks, not to mention going to the mall. But what was happening to me in the meantime? To my family? To my child? These are questions I began to ask when I realized that in addition to costing me a bundle financially, my job was costing me big-time in terms of my own and my family's needs.

WHAT DOES YOUR JOB COST YOU?

It's important when going through this calculation process to keep two things in mind: you know your own situation, and you may think of something I left out. Start with the following guidelines, and adjust them for what's true in your life:

- Make a list of all the expenses you have because you work. Include child care expenses, lunches out (but not *all* lunches out if that's something you would do anyway), gasoline, convenience foods, and especially state and federal income taxes—and don't forget the cute taxes such as Social Security, Medicare, and the like!
- Figuring out the tax rate can get very complicated. The easiest way I can think of to approximate how much is really coming out of your pay in taxes is to do the following:
  - Look at how much tax expense you and your husband have as a couple (get out last year's state and federal tax returns).
  - Recalculate the return with just your husband's salary.
  - Take the difference and divide that number by your annual salary. The resulting percentage is your own personal income tax rate.
- Have some aspirin ready in case finding out how much you really make gives you a headache.

CHAPTER 2

"BUT, I *NEED* TO WORK!"

When the well's dry, we know the worth of water.
—BENJAMIN FRANKLIN, 1746

WE ALL NEED

Babies always need something, don't they? They're either thirsty or hungry or wet or who knows what—it's always something! Of course, you and I are pretty much the same way. We all have needs that have to be met.

I've heard that the average person can survive two or three months without food, but only about four days without water. That assumes moderate weather and activity—it's a safe bet the average mother would only last a day or two!

Let's visit an average mother, and take a look at her needs of the moment. Please allow me to introduce you to Pam, who just happens to be . . .

Stranded

Pam looked nervously at her watch and shifted fourteen-month-old Stephanie onto her other hip. Almost noon. She felt little trickles of sweat forming in her armpits and on her back as she looked over her shoulder through the glass doors at the air-conditioned comfort on the other side.

I should have told them I'd be inside the store, she thought. It was too late now. All she had thought to tell the AAA operator on the phone was, "I'll be in front of Sears."

Why did this have to happen today? Pam closed her eyes against the sunlight as she fought to hold a squirming Stephanie (who was growing heavier by the minute) on her hip. *Just a quick trip to the mall for a new pair of shoes for the baby*, she thought, *and the car has to break down. On a Saturday.* Opening her eyes, she looked across the parking lot, searching for the tow truck. Stephanie pushed against her shoulder and began to cry.

"Terstee!" the baby wailed, her chubby little face turning red and blotchy.

"Okay, little one," Pam said, looking around for a bench, or even a spot of shade. She found neither. Her free hand rummaged clumsily through the diaper bag, grabbing the water bottle.

"Here you go." She popped the cap off the bottle as Stephanie took it and started drinking.

At least now she's stopped crying, Pam thought, looking around again for some shade from the summer sun.

First things first

Back in school, I remember studying a fellow named Abraham Maslow. He was a psychologist who developed a theory about what people *need* to live. He identified several areas of need that we all share: sustenance (food and water), shelter and clothing, love and acceptance, self-esteem, and self-actualization. Our friend Pam is trying to satisfy those sustenance and shelter needs for her child while she waits for the AAA truck.

Maslow called his theory a "hierarchy of needs" because he maintained that the different areas of needs must be met in a certain order. We have to build the pyramid from the bottom up. In other words, according to Maslow, before we can work on meeting our emotional needs for love and acceptance, we must first meet our physical needs for food, water, clothing, and shelter. First things first!

MASLOW'S HIERARCHY OF NEEDS

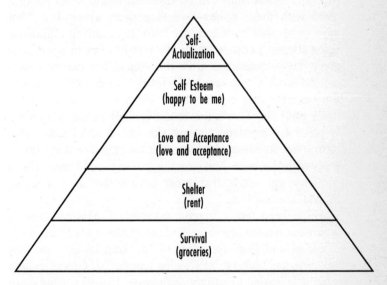

Self-Actualization

Self Esteem
(happy to be me)

Love and Acceptance
(love and acceptance)

Shelter
(rent)

Survival
(groceries)

Picture yourself stranded on a desert island (or in the Sears parking lot). You've just washed up on the shore (or the sidewalk), and you have nothing. No food, no water, no microwave! Your first concern, naturally, is survival. Let's say you are a super-duper Girl Scout and you know what to do.

You scout out a fresh water source (like the mall drinking fountain), and find some yummy berries to eat (surely there's a Taco Bell or equivalent in the food court). Congratulations! You've met Maslow's first level of needs.

Now you think of a way to fashion a posh little island shelter with some handy palm branches (if in Pam's situation, you might decide to wait *inside* the store and watch for the AAA truck from there). And a resourceful gal like you can surely create a tasteful frock from the tattered remains of a makeshift sail left on the beach by some other hapless life traveler (or the sale rack on the second floor).

You're all set! Maslow would give you an A-plus and tell you that you've accomplished (1) sustenance and (2) shelter. You're on your way up the hierarchy.

Of course, we don't have to be stranded in the Sears parking lot to deal with these issues—we face them every day. That sustenance need must be where my favorite recurring nightmare (what's for supper?) comes from. My family likes to eat practically every day—sometimes more than once! For our purposes, we'll call Maslow's "sustenance" level "groceries." I mean, even if we were living on the street, we'd still have to eat.

Shelter's obvious. That's the roof over our heads, which we keep in place by regularly paying (knock on wood) the rent/mortgage payment. Most of us spend a lot of our waking hours coming up with the money to provide groceries and rent. These are basic physical needs that must be met by all of us for survival. Maslow said so.

Once we've been fed, watered, and clothed, Maslow tells us we're ready to pursue the love and acceptance level of need. With groceries and rent taken care of, we start looking for that "special someone" who thinks we're wonderful. Groceries and rent are a little easier to satisfy than love. But if you're more than less happily mated, we'll say you've achieved love and acceptance.

So, according to Maslow, after we're fed and watered, clothed and sheltered, loved and accepted, we can begin to feel pretty good about ourselves and tackle that self-esteem level. And why not? Things are going great! We should feel good! We'll call this level "happy to be me."

But, we're not done. We haven't quite reached the top of the pyramid. We're cozy and comfy now that our physical and emotional needs have been met. We look around and ask, "What am I here for? What do I have to give the world?" And we begin to discover what makes us unique and special, those gifts that we can offer to make the world a better place. Maslow calls it "self-actualization." I call it "pretty darn rare." But hey, it can happen!

LIFE ON THE HIERARCHY

Well, we're off to a good start, but what, you may ask, does all this have to do with a mom's choice to work outside the home?

Okay, I'll tell you. Groceries and rent provide survival, or life. If you're working outside the home to provide these basic needs for your family, your choices are limited. I'm not saying that you don't have any choices, but if your job is providing the funds you need for survival, not working *may* mean not eating.

Some of you, however, may be fortunate enough to have those basic sustenance needs provided for through some other means. If you're working outside the home, chances are that your job is fulfilling some of those other needs on the old hierarchy, like acceptance or self-esteem, maybe even self-actualization.

Figuring out which needs your job is meeting for you will help you determine just how many choices you have about working. The higher you go up the hierarchy, the more choices you have. A mother working for self-esteem may decide she feels just fine, thank you, and leave her job tomorrow. A mother working for more basic needs may have to stick with a job she doesn't like just to pay the rent.

To illustrate this, I've added an inverted pyramid next to Maslow's hierarchy. The inverted pyramid represents your choices. As your physical and emotional needs are met, your choices expand. Because we all live in different circumstances, we don't all have the same options open to us.

Please don't get discouraged if you're struggling at the base

NEEDS VERSUS CHOICES

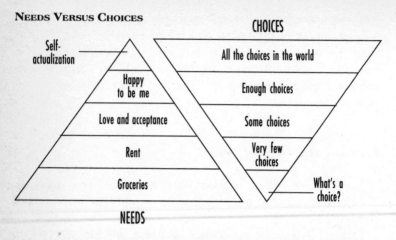

of the pyramid. Most of us work outside the home to make ends meet and pay those ever-present bills. You know, groceries, rent, car payments, credit card bills, utilities—the basics of life. The things we *need*. I mean, I really need cable TV . . . don't I?

LIFE VERSUS LIFESTYLE

Confession is supposed to be good for the soul, so I guess my soul's in for a real treat.

When I was working outside the home I really and truly believed with my whole entire being that I *needed* to work. We never seemed to have enough money. We scrambled to make ends meet, and were in debt to boot (but that didn't keep us from using our credit cards!). Besides the credit card debt we had two car payments.

On top of that we ate out almost all the time (I was usually too tired or too busy to cook), we went on frequent weekend vacations to nice, pricey locations (after all, we deserved it for working so hard—me, especially!), I had my hair cut and styled every three weeks and had my fingernails ''silk-wrapped'' (had to keep that professional look), we subscribed to cable TV (though we were hardly ever home to watch it), and I spent a lot, and I mean *a lot*, of money on clothes for my "office wardrobe."

There's probably more, but I think you get the idea, and that's about all the good my soul can stand right now.

Do you remember in Chapter One that I told you that after I adjusted my salary for taxes, day care, and other expenses, I was making about $3.50 an hour? That works out to about $600 per month, net. When I look at the list of things we spent money on while I was working, I realize that I must have spent that $600 three or four times each and every month, which put us further in debt, which strengthened my belief that I absolutely *had* to work.

I'm using myself as an example here because I don't want to pick on anyone else. You have a right to live the lifestyle of your choice, but I challenge you to ask yourself a question: Are you in control of your lifestyle, or is your lifestyle in control of you?

THE "PAY LATER" PLAN

How do you know if your lifestyle is in control of you? One sure sign that your lifestyle controls you is that you're running a balance on your credit cards. You may truly "need" to work if you have a lot of credit card bills to pay.

I think it's safe to say that as a society, we pretty much live beyond our means. Whatever we have, we want more. So we go out and get it. If we're creditworthy, we don't even need any money to get what we want. It's the "buy now, pay later" plan, and we do pay later—sometimes much, much later.

But we also pay now. It's called interest. How interesting.

You know about interest. Those are the dollars you pay each month for the privilege of carrying a balance on your credit card or paying for your car over a period of several years. Interest is part of your monthly budget if you're making payments on anything, but you probably don't think about it too much because it's just a part of the amount you owe each month. It doesn't feel like a separate thing. But it is.

Let's say (hypothetically, of course) that I buy a dress at my favorite clothing store for $80. I don't have my checkbook with me, so I utter those magic words, "Charge it," and fork over my little plastic lifestyle aid. I justify the action because I *need* that dress. Let's also say that I've repeated this ritual many times before, and I have the balance due on my credit card to prove it. I pay the minimum balance each month, so technically I won't have that dress paid for until my balance is totally paid off.

At 18 percent interest (not an uncommon credit card rate), if I take a year to pay off my balance, after adding the interest expense, that $80 dress will have cost me $87.20. If it takes me two years to pay off the balance, the dress costs me $95.05. I may not even be wearing that dress two years from now, but I could very easily still be paying for it, and the cost just keeps going up.

But it's really worse than that. The deeper you are in debt, the more using credit costs you.

Let's say (again, purely as an example) I'm making minimum payments of about $75 each month on a $3,000 credit card balance, and I'm charging about $75 every month on the card. I'm paying the same amount that I'm charging—breaking even, right? Not on your life! About $50 of that payment is interest. At the end of the year, I've made $900 in payments, but due to the magic of compounding interest, I now owe the credit card company $3,600. Hmmm. Looks like that $900 in purchases cost me $1,500 (the $900 I purchased plus the $600 additional interest that I owe on the card). So far.

JOINING THE CROWD

If you're caught in the trap described above, you are not alone. Many of us work to maintain a lifestyle financed by and provided by debt.

"My husband always says that if we made $100,000, we'd spend $150,000," said one mother while discussing her family budget. Cheri, whom we met in Chapter One, adds: "Something else that I noticed about the times that I do work outside and earn some extra money—our standard of living goes up, we spend more liberally and do not necessarily 'get ahead.' Credit cards are what killed us."

Sonya, a working mother in Indiana, agrees: "We are in the same position . . . but we realized that we had to pay for our high living of the past (pre-house and child). We won't be out of the woods for a couple of years, but [we got] those credit cards out of our wallets. . . We now live on a cash basis."

We need groceries. We need rent. We need self-esteem. But do we need to spend more on our lifestyles than we can afford? Is it possible to find a balance between what we need and what we want?

We're not the first beings on this planet to struggle with this question, as evidenced by the following:

> *Every increased possession loads us with a new weariness.*
>
> —JOHN RUSKIN, 1872

Think about it. The more "stuff" you have, the harder you have to work to maintain that "stuff." The bigger the house, the longer it takes to clean. The fancier the car, the more things on it that will break, and the more it will cost to fix them!

> *It is not the man who has too little, but the man who craves more, that is poor.*
>
> —SENECA, circa A.D. 35

It's like trying to keep up with computer technology or audio-visual equipment. It can't be done. As soon as you purchase the state-of-the-art units, they're obsolete. So you spend your time wishing you had the new stuff. You may not even enjoy the stuff you have, because you know there's something better "out there." I have a really hard time with this one. My computer software works great, but every time I hear about a new program, I want it. Just ask my husband!

> *For everything you have missed, you have gained*
> *something else; and for everything you gain, you*
> *lose something.*
> —RALPH WALDO EMERSON, 1841

Life is full of trade-offs. I don't care what anybody else says, you can't have it all! If you're working outside the home, you're giving up something neat and rewarding that could be happening in another area of your life—maybe with your kids. If you stay home and don't have a job, you may not realize the full potential of your talents.

"BUT, I WANT MORE!"

Having said all of the above, let me emphasize that there's absolutely nothing in the world wrong with working to pay for the things you want if that works for you. It can work for you, especially if you don't fall into the debt trap.

It just didn't work for me, because I wanted more than I could pay for. I poured myself into my job to the exclusion of everything and everybody else. I burdened myself with the insatiable desires of always wanting more, or better. I created "wants" so strong that I felt certain I "needed" them.

And I wasn't happy. Even though I had coifed hair and fashionable fingernails and nice clothes and weekend trips and could watch whatever I wanted to on television, I felt empty. I thought I was working for self-esteem, but at some point I quit receiving the emotional payoff.

Maybe you've been there. Maybe you are there. Maybe your job is not giving you what you need. When that happens, something's got to change.

RESCUE 911

My brother served in Vietnam. When he got home he told me the army has a rule to follow when you get wounded: If you're conscious, you're responsible for your own rescue. It doesn't matter (as was true in his case) that your body is broken in a zillion places, or you're temporarily deaf and blinded from the explosion, or you fall on your face when you try to step on the leg that just had the kneecap blown out of it.

If you're conscious, you're responsible for your own rescue.

Over the years, that rule has stuck with me. It's good advice. My job didn't fill my needs. Beyond that, I felt broken into a zillion pieces, uncertain if I could ever put my life back together again or where I would find fulfillment when I did. I realized that my preoccupation with work was causing me to lose touch with my child, and that *scared* me. But I was conscious, so I was responsible for my own rescue.

I decided to come home. That meant giving up some of the "extras" which I had defined before as "needs." We cut back on expenses. Now when we watch television, it's a local station (often fuzzy). We started paying cash and put away the credit cards. I let my hair grow and I enjoy "natural" fingernails. And I cook—more or less.

I have less now, but at the same time, I have more. I have more peace about who I am and what I'm doing with my life. I have more time with my son, and to pursue the things *I* want to do—like writing. I have a more relaxed home, and, yes, more dirty dishes (from all that cooking). But I also have more compassion for my husband and the hard work he does, because I know what it's like out there.

NEEDS OR WANTS?

Yes, it's easy to fool ourselves into thinking we need to work, when what we really need is to reexamine our priorities.

And sometimes, many times, we confuse the things we *want* with the things we *need*.

There are many things about our lives that we can control. We can make choices about our lifestyles, and we do make those choices every day. If we take an honest look at what our choices have been up to now, we may even discover that we need less than we thought.

Up to this point, we've talked only about our own needs. There are, however, other people in our lives who have needs. We'll call these people "children."

CHAPTER 3 ✑

GUILT—I MEAN, CHILDREN

(No book for mothers would be complete
without it.)

*"Immediately following birth, every new
mother drags from her bed and awkwardly
pulls herself up on the pedestal provided for
her."*

—ERMA BOMBECK, 1983

PACK YOUR BAGS—WE'RE GOING ON A GUILT TRIP!

The way I figure it, we might as well straighten out this guilt
thing right here and now. Something happens to us when we
become mothers—and it isn't pretty. Our guilt glands swell up.
(I'm not a doctor, but I believe those particular glands are lo-
cated in the hip, thigh, and buttocks areas.)

We all feel guilty. Every last loving one of us.

It's easy to see why we feel guilty about our kids—raising
them is such a tremendous responsibility! It weighs on us. We
worry that we're doing the wrong things—scarring them for
life—giving them stories to tell their therapists in twenty years
(while praying that there truly is such a thing as "forgive and
forget").

Every time I yell at—I mean, unfairly correct—Ryan because
I'm tired, I feel guilty. If he gets hurt when I'm not with him,

I feel guilty. (I should have been there!) If he gets hurt and I *am* there, I feel guilty. (I should have prevented it!)

And our kids are smart. They figure out at a very early age the dynamics of the guilt trip, and exactly how to give Mommy a one-way ticket. In some circles this innate ability of children is called "pushing your buttons." If you've ever had your buttons pushed, you know what I'm talking about: the well-timed tear, the pouty lip, the "humph" you hear as your child dejectedly leaves the room. Then there are the phrases that we've come to know and fear: "All the other kids have one!" "But you *promised*!" "You don't LOVE me!"

A NOTE TO THOSE IN DENIAL

I've been around the block enough times to know that there is a gentle reader somewhere whose eyebrows are raised on what she considers to be a guilt-free face. "The stimulation of day care is wonderful—even for babies!" she may be thinking, or "I don't feel guilty—who does she think she is—trying to make me feel guilty!" Right now it's very important for that reader to know that I'm not trying to make anyone feel anything, or *do* anything for that matter.

My mother once gave me some very good advice, so I'll pass it along to you: Never buy anyone's whole package. What that means is, you may not agree with everything I have to say here, but there still might be some information you'll find useful. If you *don't* feel guilty, write me and tell me how you escaped this mother's malady! But I'm certain you know someone who feels guilty about her kids, so you can read the rest of this chapter with her in mind. Who knows, you may even find one or two things you like for yourself.

We're bombarded daily by a variety of guilt inducers: well-meaning mothers and mothers-in-law, stay-at-home moms who seem to have it all together, working moms who appear to be ultra-organized, *any* mom whose kids aren't having problems when ours are, perfect television moms, moms in commercials who buy the right kind of juice . . . well, you know what I mean.

Let's visit a mother who's dealing with some guilt issues just about now. She's . . .

Doing the Best She Can

Melanie carefully separated Mrs. Freemont's hair into the neat sections she would roll up for the perm. She'd been on her feet for hours, was running behind, and could see that her 4:30 was already seated in the waiting room, frowning at the digital wall clock that glowed 4:35.

Melanie took a deep breath and convinced herself to smile.

"We're using the pink rods today, right?" she asked the elderly lady seated in front of the mirror.

"Oh, no, I don't think so," Mrs. Freemont answered. Her right hand cupped the dripping gray hair. "We did pink last time, and I *told* you the curl didn't keep. You said I'd do better with blue or maybe even yellow!" The irritation on her face reflected back at Melanie from the mirror.

"Well, blue, maybe," Melanie replied, trying to keep her smile alive. "Yellow might give you a tighter curl than you'd like. Why don't we go with the blue today, and see how that works for you?"

Before Mrs. Freemont had a chance to respond, Claire called out from the front desk, "Melanie, phone call!"

"Excuse me just a minute." Melanie walked over to the phone with some relief, but just when Claire handed her the receiver, she saw 4:30 looking at her watch. Pulling the receiver to her ear, she turned away and faced the wall of hair care products opposite the desk.

"Mel?" the voice on the phone said.

"Hi, Mom," answered Melanie when she heard her mother's familiar voice. "What's the matter? Is Missy okay?"

"It's almost five. Your father called and he wants me home to cook dinner. When are you coming home?"

"It's gonna be at least a quarter to six before I get out of here," Melanie said. "Can't you wait just a little while longer?"

"No, I can't. I'm just going to have to take Missy with me—again. I don't know why you have to have that job anyway, when you should be home taking care of your daughter."

Melanie sighed. "Mom, we've been all through this. I don't want Missy growing up with a mother on welfare," she said. "I want her to learn that people have to work for what they get."

"A child needs her mother. Missy's been crying for you all day long—driving me crazy! I was always there for you."

You had Daddy, Melanie thought. "Listen, I can't talk about it right now. Just take her with you and I'll come pick her up when I'm done here."

"That child needs her mother," Melanie's mom repeated, then hung up the phone.

Placing the receiver back in its cradle, Melanie felt the weight of her mother's words. She had been tempted, when Brian left, to take her mother's advice and live on government assistance. But she knew, deep in her heart, the best thing she could do for her three-year-old daughter was to get a job, and try to make some kind of life for the two of them.

Melanie looked up and caught 4:30's eye. "I'll be with you in about fifteen minutes," she said, smiling.

Back at her station, Melanie bent over to pull the basket of blue perm rods from under the counter. She felt a lump rise in her throat when she stood up and saw Missy's picture taped to the mirror. But she forced another smile and started rolling.

Do you feel guilty or what?

Melanie's fending off the guilt her mother is trying to send her way, and it's true that much of the guilt we feel is triggered by others. But I'd be willing to bet that the guilt we experience at the hands of our kids and other "well-meaning" folks is *nothing* compared to the way we beat up on ourselves!

As I listened to mothers across America discussing this subject, I heard some evidence of these "self-inflicted" guilt wounds. How many of the following statements strike a chord with you?

I feel guilty because:

- My family never eats dinner together.
- I feel out of touch with my kids.
- I'm missing my baby's milestones.
- My child cries when I leave him at day care.
- My older kids are missing after-school activities because I can't take them.
- I'm not "there" for my child.
- I *have* to work and I'd rather be at home.
- I really enjoy my work and sometimes I think I should want to be home.
- I spoil my kids to make up for not being with them.
- When I was home on maternity leave, I couldn't wait to get back to work.

When we feel guilty about our kids, it's because we hear a little voice somewhere saying, "You *should* be with your kids." That little voice might be inside our own heads, or it might be the very audible voice of one of those "well-meaning" people in our lives.

At the same time, we moms (and all women, for that matter) are hearing other voices: "Don't waste yourself at home!" "Develop your gifts!" "Pay the light bill!"

Geez. No wonder we're so confused. Who knows what to think with all these voices telling us all these different things? And they are all talking at the same time.

So just what are we supposed to do with these guilt feelings? How do we deal with the guilt that inevitably plagues us as mothers?

Maybe the first thing we need to do is examine those feelings and decide if "guilt" is what we're actually experiencing, or if some other emotions are mixed in there as well.

"I work because I have to in order to provide food and shelter for my three-year-old son," says Rhonda in Illinois. "I still feel really guilty more often than not. I have pictures of him all over my desk at work from the day he was born."

Boy, can I relate to that. I had pictures all over my desk of my son, too. I used to gaze at that sweet little photogenic face and feel my heart go pitter-patter, then I'd sigh and get back to work.

I wanted to be with him. I felt guilty because I wasn't with him.

I would rush to the day care after work to take my child into my loving arms so we could go home and experience "quality time" together. I can still remember those joyful reunions . . .

I arrive at the day care, sign Ryan out for the day, and pick up his backpack and lunchpail from the nearby cubby. At this time of day the kids are playing outside, so I head out to the playground to find him. I scan the crowd for a bouncing blond head. There! There he is!

"Ryan," I call, waving and smiling.

My son, caught in the middle of a fun game, pretends not to see me. He runs away.

I walk over to the crowd of children, stepping gingerly in my heels over the sandy ground.

*"Come on, Ryan, it's time to go home," my voice
rings sweetly across the playground.*
    Ryan runs gleefully in the opposite direction.
    *"Ryan!" Sweetness gone, replaced by irritation.
"It's time to go home!"*
    *The giggling boy finally bounces in my direction.
"I don't wanna go home," he tells me. "Can you
come back later?"*

Looking back, I wonder—was what I was feeling guilt? Or
did I just *miss* my child? Was leaving him in day care what I
felt guilty about?

IS IT GUILT—OR SOMETHING ELSE?

Jenny, a single mother of a three-year-old son, struggled in frustration when picking him up from day care.
He "kicked and screamed" all the way to the car.

   She met with the day care director. "I feel so guilty!"
she cried. "He's so unhappy!" For a while, she tried
spending her lunch hour with the three-year-old, but
that, too, was a disaster. Her noontime visits only
seemed to upset him more.

   Finally, Jenny tried a new approach. When she arrived at the day care center in the evening, she didn't
try to rush her son home. Instead, she spent some time
with him and let him "finish up" his play activity. Often
they shared a snack together as he got used to the
idea of leaving the center and going home. Finally, after
other children had begun to leave and things had qui-
eted down, he was ready to go.

   "It made all the difference in the world," says the day
care director. "Mother and child left for home happy and
relaxed, well worth the additional fifteen to twenty
minutes."

"OTHER" CARE

What we're talking about here is the question of what happens to our kids when we're not with them.

This is where you might expect to read about the results of studies done by psychologists and other experts about the harmful effects of day care on children. You might even be bracing yourself for the onslaught of statistics detailing the ruination of the nation's children. If you're *really* interested in feeling guilty, go ahead and check out some of those studies at the library. They are guaranteed guilt-inducers.

But what we're dealing with here is figuring out what works best for *you* and *your family*. The only way you can do that is to look at your own kids and how they are *actually* doing. I've talked to too many working moms whose children didn't become axe murderers to believe that day care, *in and of itself*, is a negative thing for our kids to experience. Besides, as Betty Holcomb noted in her July 1994 article in *Working Mother* magazine, "How Families Are Changing for the Better," "Researchers have not found any evidence that the mere fact that a mother is employed has negative consequences for her children or her marriage."

Anyway, day care isn't the only care alternative for working mothers. I was surprised to learn that many working mothers employ nannies, or au pairs, to provide child care in their own homes. And some people have the luxury of a grandma nearby who helps while mom works. Still others work out coordinating schedules with their husbands so that one parent is with the children at any given time.

Whatever situation you and your kids find yourselves in, your assignment (if you will) is to take an honest look at how your kids are functioning in their care environment. The key word here is "honest." If you take that look and find that your children are thriving, maybe some of those guilt feelings will go away. If the picture you see is something other than happy, healthy kids—well, you're going to have to do something about it, aren't you?

Looking back at the time my son was in day care, I can see that my feelings of guilt were misplaced. He loved day care. They played games. They made "gooey-goo." Who wouldn't love that?

If I'm really honest with myself, I have to admit that what I felt guilty about had nothing to do with leaving him in day care. No, my feelings of guilt came from a source much closer to home.

QUALITY TIME

Don't you just *hate* that phrase? I do. Maybe I hate it because I'm not very good at making it happen.

For example, my "quality time" with Ryan consisted of the few minutes we had together in the car between the day care and home. Once home, exhausted, I set about scrounging something for dinner or ordering a pizza. I ushered Ryan in front of the television for a video game or movie. Or if our busy family had something scheduled for the evening, I herded him into the bathroom for an early bath. When my husband arrived home I "debriefed" my day to him—all the things that had happened at work. This sometimes took hours.

After dinner, too physically and emotionally exhausted to do anything else, I watched TV and tried to forget about work. At the appropriate time I sent Ryan to bed. Sometimes I took him, sometimes I didn't.

In short, my priority evening activity was *rest and recovery*, not spending time with my son. I can't count the number of times I said to him, "Mommy's too tired" when he asked me to play a game or take him to bed. Often my mind drifted to the things I needed to accomplish the next day at the office. My job definitely came first in my life, and my energies were all directed toward that priority.

If someone had asked me to make a list of my priorities, I'm sure my son would have been right up there at the top. But if someone asked me to make a list of my activities, a record of how I actually spent my time, the entries including Ryan would have been (and were) few and far between.

Fortunately, there are working mothers out there who still manage to give their kids what they need. Just listen to what Marsha, a mom in Illinois, shared with me about her mother:

> *I think there's a big difference in kids who know that their parents didn't have a choice about working and those who have parents on the fast track. I am the daughter of a now-deceased alcoholic father who spent his pay on drinks. Mom kept us afloat. She was uneducated as far as formal schooling goes but worked assembly lines and soldering in factories all her life.*
>
> *Mom had to work six days a week and we didn't have material things. But she would lie down after work with us next to her and she would talk to and with us. She would rub my head just so—I can remember even now how it felt. We didn't know, then, that she just needed to lie down. To us it was just special.*

Some of us make time for our kids. Some of us don't. Our kids either make it with what we give them, or they don't. Are your kids making it?

You're the only person who can answer that question.

POSITIVELY GUILTY

Okay, a lot of us feel guilty—agreed. But what are we going to do about it? I've always believed if there's something in life that you can't get out of, you might as well make the best of it. So I try to enjoy dishes and laundry. It doesn't always work, but it's a good philosophy—worth the effort, anyway!

We can make the best out of our feelings of guilt by listening to what those feelings are telling us. If those feelings are telling us that we really could be doing more for our kids, then we can begin to work toward that goal. We can decide whether our actions line up with our priorities. And if they don't, we can make positive changes.

We may find that we're feeling guilty because for years someone else has been telling us that we *should*. In that case, maybe it's time to invest in a little therapy. Whatever we find, it's up to each one of us to do something about it.

CHILDREN AND CHOICES

Pardon me if I get serious for a minute. Many people will argue vehemently that a mother belongs in the home with her children, that a working mom is at best a "second-best" choice. But I believe that the key to making choices that involve our children is to recognize and take responsibility for how those choices affect our children. Many working mothers manage very well, without leaving deep psychological scars on their kids. I've listened to many adult children of working moms who, like Marsha, are proud of their mothers, and didn't feel slighted because Mom had responsibilities outside the home. So I know it's possible for kids to survive, and even thrive, with a mother who works outside the home.

At the same time, I'm aware of families where Mom works and it doesn't work for the kids. The children in these families are lost, often do poorly in school, or gain attention from their parents the only way they know how—by getting into trouble. My own situation was one in which my choice to work outside the home did not work for my child's emotional health and well-being. He needed more from me than I could give while I was so wrapped up in my job. For me, and my child, the job had to go.

So why does working work for some people and not for others? Why can some of us successfully work outside the home, while some of us, for our own and our family's well-being, need to stay home?

The answer is simple, as answers to questions of this type usually are. We are each different, and our kids are different. Some of us have children who need more of our time, our physical presence, than others. Some moms are good at handling the responsibilities of a job without slighting their children. Others (like me) seem to be able to handle only one or two responsibilities at a time.

The trick, then, is to make the *right* choice about working, given what both we and our children need. It doesn't make any sense to achieve all the financial or emotional success in the world if our children aren't going to make it without us. At the same time, it doesn't make any sense to "sacrifice" our talents and be miserable at home—if we might then take out our misery and frustration on our kids.

Take an honest look at your kids. How are they doing—really? Take responsibility for what you see. If you see something that needs to change, have the courage to make that change. For some that will mean leaving the working world. For others it will mean trying to manage your work and family responsibilities more efficiently.

Which means you may want to sign up for the upcoming course, Juggling 101.

CHAPTER 4 ∾

JUGGLING 101

My candle burns at both ends;
It will not last the night.
                    —EDNA ST. VINCENT MILLAY, 1920

COURSE DESCRIPTION

Juggling 101 is offered to help working mothers manage time and responsibilities in a satisfying way that will promote better mental health through more efficient use of energy, money, and time, including, but not limited to, additional benefits such as weight loss, an improved sex life, and a noticeable increase in good hair days.*

LESSON ONE—DEFINING THE TERMS

Okay, class, today we're going to start with some basic definitions on the subject of juggling. Let's see what Mr. Webster has to say on the subject:

---

*As with any self-improvement program, participants are advised to seek the advice of their doctor or mental health professional before implementing the activities outlined in the course. If, after doing this, you really expect the aforementioned benefits, see me after class—I have a piece of swamp property you may want to purchase.

juggle—to *perform tricks* of *dexterity*, esp. to throw several objects into the air one after another, catching them and throwing them again, repeatedly and rhythmically without a pause to make complex, confusing play.

Well! I don't know about you, but I'm tempted to say, "Enough said!" That definition pretty much describes my life when I was working outside the home—you know, the job, driving to school, doing the laundry, exercise, Little League, getting dinner together, going to the grocery store, taking clothes to the dry cleaners, birthday parties (and let's *not* forget shopping for clothing) . . . repeatedly and rhythmically without pause . . . yes, juggle. I *know* this term. But just what does Webster mean by "perform"?

perform—to do, fulfill, carry out (. . . an obligation), accomplish, to render, execute, esp. before an audience.

Carry out an obligation . . . especially before an audience. Yep—sounds familiar. Next?

trick—. . . a dexterous feat intended to puzzle or cause wondering admiration, . . . an inexplicable process . . . the special techniques that constitute the expertise of an experienced craftsman.

Oh, yes, yes! I like the part about causing wondering admiration. And making life happen for my family is *definitely* an inexplicable process. Oh, and that part about having special techniques and expertise . . . makes me tingle! Give me more, Websty, give me more!

dexterity—manual skill, deftness, mental adroitness.

Wait a minute—I'm supposed to do all this wonderfu
and *think*, too? Maybe I'd better look up "adroit" and '

> *adroit*—dexterous, nimble, lively, and resourceful in
> dealing with difficult situations or people.

Well, I agree that today's working mother must be resourceful in difficult situations. But what's this business about being
nimble and lively? Are we possibly getting a little carried away
here? I mean, what's wrong with "conscious and breathing"?
Give me a break!

> *deft*—quick and neat, clever, quick-witted.

Quick? Neat? Clever? This is too much! Help! (But hurry. I
need to be somewhere in ten minutes.)

LESSON TWO—WHAT THEY DON'T TELL YOU

Well, class, I don't know about you, but just reading those
definitions wears me out. That's one thing Webster didn't tell
us: Juggling makes us tired. All that "repeatedly and rhythmically without pause" stuff is what does it. You know what I
mean—moving from one obligation to the next, all day long
and into the night, trying to keep all the balls in the air. And
if you happen to drop a ball now and again, you just hope and
pray it's not a big one that'll bounce back up in your face and
mess up your mascara.

No one told me it was going to be like this. They don't, you
know. They don't tell you how hard it's going to be to have
kids, let alone to have kids *and* a job *and* take care of yourself
and your home and *maybe* even talk to your husband once in
a while.

No. They don't tell you the things you really need to know.
They let you find out for yourself. Some people call it the

"school of hard knocks," which is another way of saying, "Hey! I suffered through this so you have to suffer, too!"

Well, I don't happen to agree with that "hard knocks" philosophy, so I'm going to tell.

To begin with, when you combine motherhood with working outside the home, you can kiss your social life goodbye. This is really a tough one, because to be healthy, happy, balanced, and all that neat stuff, you really need to have friends in your life. But it's hard for a working-outside-the-home mom to accomplish this. Says Robin: "Though I desperately want friends, I have very little time for them. And baby-sitters are expensive, especially when you've already paid for child care for two during the day."

Often a working mom's social life centers around, or is limited to, her family. And even husband-wife "dates" can be rare. Chris, a mom in New Jersey, agrees. "Our family is basically our social life. There's so little time with the kids that I hate to leave them with a sitter. We do try to go out once a month, just the two of us."

Here's something else they don't tell you: Women are still doing most of the housework. We don't like to hear that, because of the women's movement and everything, but it's true. Just listen to what Dr. Maisha Hamilton Bennett, head of Hamilton Behavioral Health Care in Chicago, said on the subject in a May 1994 *Ebony* article entitled "The Working Mother's Dilemma":

> *Women have always shouldered the lion's share of the responsibility for the home and hearth. And that situation didn't change much after the Women's Liberation Movement sent scores of women out in search of outside employment; their job and career duties were just tacked onto their list of things to do.*

It's sad, but true. One of the reasons we have such a hard time juggling everything is that we're doing most of the work at home plus the work at work. It's two jobs in one mom!

University of Akron sociologist Patricia Ulbrich conducted a survey that reports that women, whether or not we have a job outside the home, do 32.3 hours of housework a week. (Personally, I'm doing everything that I possibly can to bring the average down!) That's almost as many hours as we spend working in a full-time job! No wonder we get so tired.

Do you remember that song from a few years back about how we women can "bring home the bacon and fry it up in the pan"? We thought we could do it all, but I ask you, what's so great about that? Why on earth would we want to do it all? In my dream life, someone else does all the stuff I don't want to do—like cooking dinner and scrubbing toilets. I've never wanted to do it all!

THE SPUD STOPS HERE

"We may have come a long way, baby, but 80 percent of the women in dual-income households are still in charge of dinner—day in and day out," reports Marty Meitus of the *Pittsburgh Post-Gazette* (June 8, 1994).

Such were the results of a survey conducted by Ketchum Communications for the National Potato Board. The national telephone survey included responses from five hundred women, as well as focus-group studies in four cities.

The survey found that women overwhelmingly retain meal preparation responsibility, "despite time pressures equal to or more demanding than men."

Not surprising, but definitely "food for thought."

Before any irate readers throw down this book in disgust because I have neglected to mention that some husbands do actually help with the housework, let me point out that some husbands do actually help with the housework. Mine does. Back in my employed days, if it had not been for Arnold's help in the kitchen, I would have converted our family completely to disposable dining: people huddled over the kitchen sink balancing fast food on paper plates and drinking directly from milk cartons, because the table was always full of whatever each of us brought home at the end of the day. Not a pretty picture. No, he saved us from all that by helping me keep up with the kitchen.

(Now that I'm working at home, we eat our fast food sitting at the table, on real dishes. But I digress.)

My husband has also been known to vacuum, dust, and do the laundry, and he even irons his own shirts!

So you can understand why it didn't take long for him to suggest to me that we hire a maid. Isn't that great? My dream was coming true!

No one told me that I'd have to clean the house before the maid came (so that she could *find* the toilets). Oh, well. It was a nice dream while it lasted.

LESSON THREE—MULTI-TASKING

Computers are great! Mine can do several things at once. I can use the word processor for my writing while another area of the computer checks the e-mail. I can play a computer game while I'm waiting for a chapter to print out, or even balance my checkbook (which is on the computer, too), or work on another chapter at the same time. It's all very efficient. This ability to jump almost seamlessly from one program to another is called multi-tasking.

Let's bring this whole juggling issue into the nineties. What we're really talking about here is learning to do multi-tasking. Like a computer, we need to be able to overlap our activities in such a way that everything gets done—with seamless efficiency. You know, things like taking your kids with you on errands you have to do anyway. You can talk with them while driving from place to place, plus spend time together. Or when you can't sleep because all that ''job'' stuff keeps running through your head, fold the laundry or pick up that book you've been trying to get around to reading.

I sometimes used to put the finishing touches on my makeup in the car while driving to work. But since that process was neither seamless nor efficient, maybe it doesn't qualify here. Also, I should mention that if you have trouble walking and chewing gum at the same time, get into this multi-tasking thing slowly. We don't want anyone to get hurt.

Please understand that just because I'm comparing us moms to computers, I don't expect us to reach perfection in our ability to multi-task. Even computers aren't perfect. Mine often locks up and refuses to do anything at all, especially if I've given it too many commands at once. Computers have their limits—just as we do! When faced with a never-ending list of Important Things to Do Right This Very Minute, I've been known to lock up on several occasions. Just shut down. Someone comes in when I'm already up to my eyeballs in work, and tells me he needs something right away. And all I can do is give him a blank stare with my head cocked to one side.

When a computer locks up, the only thing you can do to fix it is push the reset button, or turn the whole thing off and just start all over again. In computerese it's called rebooting. Sometimes this is exactly what we need, too: reset, take a break, start over. Being able to multi-task, or juggle, doesn't mean that we have to do it perfectly all the time, despite what Webster says about "repeatedly and rhythmically without a pause." We just do the best we can until things start to fall apart, then we start all over again. That's normal.

One morning I was taking Ryan to school on my way to work. I have a bad habit of rushing out of the house without everything I need, then about three blocks down the road I remember "whatever." With a sigh and, usually, a growl, I turn around and go home to get "whatever."

But this particular morning, when I remembered "whatever," I didn't have time to turn around and go home. So I did the next best thing: I started to chew myself out.

"I can't *believe* I forgot that!" I exclaimed, harshly. "I *can't believe* I *did* that!'' After fuming for a few more seconds, I exploded, "*I can't believe I forgot that again!*" Then I turned to Ryan, who was sitting next to me looking for the nearest exit, and as calmly as I could, explained that I was not mad at him, I was mad at myself because I *forgot* what I needed *again*! (Which only got me started all over.)

Ryan, wise beyond his then seven years, looked over at me and said, "Mommy, I think you're pushing yourself over the edge!"

He was right, of course. Hearing him say that caught me so off-guard that I burst out laughing, and we enjoyed the rest of the trip to school. His little comment was the "boot" I needed to reset my attitude.

There's one other thing that happens with my computer that applies to this lesson. Every once in a while, I try to launch a program and this message appears on the screen: *Cannot execute this program from a multi-tasking environment.* Some programs are very particular about sharing their space—they simply won't! And there are some things in my life (and yours) that I can't (and shouldn't) do while trying to accomplish a myriad of other tasks.

One such time is during emergencies. If I'm taking someone to the hospital, I just don't seem to worry whether the dishes have been done. Other activities in my life cannot happen in a multi-tasking environment, such as when Arnold and I need private time together. (I don't think I need to spell that one out for you.) And there are times that Ryan needs my absolute and undivided attention. None of these activities can function properly within a multi-tasking environment. Sometimes I just have to let go of everything and focus on that one very important item, and let the chips fall where they may.

LESSON FOUR—PEOPLE DO WHAT THEY CHOOSE TO DO

Once my mother called and asked if I could come visit her in Houston. "Oh, I couldn't possibly this weekend," I answered. "I'm far too busy."

"People do what they choose to do," my mother said.

At first I was offended. I thought she was trying to make me feel guilty. But later, as I reflected on her comment, I realized that she was right. I could have gone to Houston, if that was what I really wanted to do. I mean, if she had told me that my father was dying in the hospital, I would have gone without a second thought. The fact was that I chose to do the things I had already planned. I *chose* not to change those plans because I didn't want to.

People do what they choose to do.

Think about it. This is important. Each day, as we're faced with all the tasks we have to juggle, don't we pick and choose the ones we want to do, and let the others fall by the wayside?

People do what they choose to do.

Oh, I hear you. Someone out there is saying, "I don't *choose* to pay the bills, I *have* to!"

To which I calmly respond, you don't *have* to pay the bills. You choose to pay the bills because you're responsible. But you don't *have* to. In fact, lots of people don't pay their bills!

Some of us are a little hesitant about admitting that we do what we choose to do, because then we'll have to take responsibility for those choices. It's much easier to "blame" our choices on someone else (the old "devil made me do it" defense), but it isn't true.

We do what we choose to do.

Now, I'm not talking here about things that *happen to us*. I'm not talking about acts of God, like earthquakes and floods and tornadoes. (If insurance policies can exclude those things, so can I.) Neither am I talking about things that happen to us because of the actions of other people. No one chooses to be burgled or to have her car smashed from behind. We don't have control over other people any more than we have control over the forces of nature.

But I do have control over me. And you have control over you. And we do what we choose to do.

Now that that's established, the next thing to remember is: Do what you're doing.

In other words, once you've chosen what you're going to do, do it! Don't monkey around pretending you're not going to do it. Sometimes people hold back because they're afraid they're choosing the wrong things—they don't want to make any mistakes or be embarrassed. I was in a choir once, in which the director told us, "If you're going to make a mistake, make it with confidence!" That was one of the best choirs I sang with. It's amazing what you can accomplish when you give it all you've got.

Taking responsibility for our own choices is the only way we can ever hope to become successful jugglers. We can read books about getting organized. We can go to time management seminars. We can find out how someone else got organized. We can listen to everyone who promises to make our lives easier or more productive. We want to manage all the pressures we experience in our lives—so we keep looking for answers.

But the best we can hope to learn from other people is *what worked for them*. We're still responsible for figuring out what's going to work for us.

In a way, this entire book is about becoming a successful juggler, because it's about choosing the life that works for you. What kind of life are you choosing?

We do what we choose to do.

FINAL EXAM

In review, class, the purpose of the course is to encourage you to make the choices that work for you. The final exam, therefore, can be graded only by you. You determine how honest you can be with yourself, and whether you have passed the course. I advise you to answer the questions carefully, and honestly. This is probably the only final exam you will ever take in which it is okay to get the answers from a whispering voice—as long as that voice is your own. Get out your no. 2 pencil—and good luck!

JUGGLING 101 FINAL EXAMINATION

1. *True or False:*

I should try to do everything everyone expects me to.

2. Successful juggling is:

      (a) the art of causing wondering amazement.
      (b) different for each person.
      (c) multi-tasking.
      (d) All of the above.

3. (Essay question.) Finish the following sentence:

If I were to *choose* to do what I *really want* to do with my life, I would. . .

CHAPTER 5

THE FATHER FACTOR

(What—someone *else* has an opinion?)

Hear the other side.
—Saint Augustine, circa a.d. 400

What's wrong with this picture?

I'm flipping through a major women's magazine, a magazine that focuses on mothers who work outside the home. I like the magazine. I like how it deals with the issues we moms face. In the front part of this particular issue, I notice a letter from the editor. At the top of the letter I see a quarter-page photo of Mom (AKA "editor"), child one, child two—and the family dog. Period.

What really catches my attention is the dog. I've seen countless photos like this in magazines for us hard-working moms. Mom and child(ren) in the den. Mom and child(ren) at the office. Mom and child(ren) at the park. Over and over again. It isn't until I see *this* picture, the one with the dog, that I ask myself, "Where's Dad?"

I'm thinking, *Maybe she's a single mom.* That would explain why the family dog is in the picture and Dad isn't. So, with mounting curiosity, I read the letter. Toward the end of the letter, Mom (AKA "editor") mentions a husband. *Aha*, I think, *he exists!*

So why isn't he in the picture?

MAKING ROOM FOR DADDY

I suppose there are all kinds of reasons why that particular dad wasn't in that particular photograph. He was at work when they did the shoot. He's shy. He looks so much like the family dog, he didn't think anyone would notice if he wasn't there. He's a member of a religious group that doesn't believe in photographs. He's in the government's witness protection program and can't risk exposure. Yes, any number of possibilities exist.

But I *suspect* that he wasn't in the picture for one very essential reason: It simply isn't done.

We moms, especially when we're publicly talking about us and ours, don't like to mention the possibility that perhaps, just perhaps, many of us don't do this parenting thing alone. We may want Dad to help out with the kids and the housework, but we're not very quick to give him credit for it. If we do, somebody might think we're weak, or unessential, or incapable of handling anything and everything that life throws at us.

Oh, we talk among ourselves about our children's fathers. We tell one another what he did, and what he didn't do, and what we wish he'd do, and what we're going to do if he doesn't do it. We might even bring him up in an occasional article for mothers—but don't, for heaven's sake, take his picture.

I wasn't even going to mention much about fathers here, for the same reasons. I mean, we're talking about mothers, right? But the more I researched, the more these fathers kept popping up. It's like they're real people or something. They love their kids. They have opinions about where we moms work. Go figure.

Whether or not we acknowledge them, fathers are very much in the picture. If we moms have a choice to work outside the home, it's likely there's a father out there somewhere providing for the family financially. And in this world of changing roles, fathers face some of the same work versus family choices that we've been talking about. Because we have this in common with them, and because their attitudes, feelings, and opinions can greatly affect the choices open to us moms, we're going to "make room for the daddies" and talk about them for a while.

Still, it's difficult to know where to begin. Fathers are so fascinatingly faceted, we could go on and on . . . but, hey, let's stick with the basics. Fathers are people. I want to make this one point very clear, because just like us, each one of them is different. And because they are each different, our choices as mothers are affected in different ways, depending on the father we're dealing with. I'm not an expert when it comes to fathers—far from it! But I am clear on this one thing. Fathers are people.

Let's use that as a starting place, and see where we end up.

FATHER FACT:
In a 1989 *USA Today* poll, 74 percent of the men who responded said they would trade a slower career track for more family time.

PEOPLE HAVE OPINIONS

"I'd like to work," one mom told me, "and I did work when we were first married. But when our first baby was born my husband said I had to quit. He really feels strongly about a mom staying home with the kids."

"I'm very lucky that my husband helps with the morning

routine," another mom shares. "I take the baby to day care on the way to work and he gets the older child dressed and to the school bus before he leaves. He's very supportive!"

Let's see. This is pretty basic. Fathers are people. People have opinions. Therefore, fathers have opinions.

I'll just bet your husband has an opinion or two. (And please, when I use the word "husband," I'm referring to "him," that guy in your life. Let's not argue over semantics just because you may call your guy something other than husband. Work with me here, okay?) Anyway, your husband may have very strong "don't argue with me" opinions about whether the mother of his children is going to get a job or stay home with the kids. And, contrary to popular belief, I'm here to tell you that his opinion counts.

Before anyone starts throwing spit-wads at me, let's talk about change for a minute, because change is a big piece of the opinion puzzle these days. Our male/female roles are changing. A lot of us, men and women alike, aren't quite sure how we fit in with all the changes—and all the available options. The old, standard definitions of who does what, when, and where, are gone. Men struggle with these changes the same way we do.

Of course, some things will never change. When it comes to making babies, men provide the sperm and women get to give birth. That's pretty much set in stone, even allowing for scientific advances. Men will always lose weight ten times faster than women, with half the effort. Women will always hate them for it. These things we can count on to ground us in reality for years to come.

But who does what, when it comes to moms and dads, isn't set in stone. At least not anymore. And your husband's opinions about his changing role in the family—and yours—will very much affect the choices you make.

I know. This isn't what you wanted to hear. You want me to tell you that you are your own woman and you don't have to check in with anyone before you do what you want to do.

Well, I'm not going to say that—because if you're a married person, it simply isn't true.

I am making some assumptions here. I'm assuming you care enough about your husband to be at least a little interested in his opinion. I'm also assuming you want a healthy, happy relationship with him. Assumption number three is that he's not the enemy. He is, after all, the person you chose to be with.

Okay. Let's review. A father is a person. He has opinions. His opinions count.

Follow?

FATHER FACT:
Fathers never baby-sit; they parent.

SHE SAYS, HE SAYS

Now we get to the meat of the matter: What kinds of opinions does your husband have about where you work? Can you talk to him about it? Have you asked him how he feels? I like to ask my husband what he thinks. Then I do what I want. Sometimes I do what I want before I ask for his opinion. Okay. Sometimes I don't ask. I just "do."

Now, I understand completely that the women's movement tells us that we need to make our own decisions and fulfill our own destinies and all that stuff. That's fine and good if you live in a vacuum. (Personally, I try to avoid vacuums if at all possible.) But when there are other people in your life—and we have agreed that fathers are people—making decisions about where we work involves more than just deciding on our own what works best for us. We need input from those other people.

The difficulty here is that sometimes it's hard to talk to our husbands because we communicate in different ways. For example, the other night Arnold and I were having a typical conversation:

"Remember that antique store we went to on our honeymoon—the one in Fredericksburg?" I asked.

"That was on Wednesday, right?" he answered.

"I don't know," I said. I don't care, I thought. *"Do you remember the store?"*

"Which one? We went to a lot of antique stores."

"Oh, you know. That one with all the washstands. That really neat antique store."

"We didn't go there until Thursday."

"What does that have to do with anything? Do you remember the store or not?"

"No. Wait. It was Wednesday. Yeah, I'm sure it was Wednesday."

We've been known to go on like this, sometimes, for hours. As much as I want him to, Arnold can't read my mind and "know" which antique store I'm thinking of. I'm really not interested in which day of the week we were there. To him that's a vital piece of the puzzle. Men are more tactile than we are—more grounded in the concrete (which may explain why we sometimes feel like we're talking to a brick wall). They are interested in things they can see, hold, throw, hammer and eat. They like to conquer things. It's their special way.

Communicating successfully with your husband about your feelings means putting things in terms that he can understand. One mom drew a football diagram of the house: The "X" was her husband taking care of the baby in the nursery, and the "O" was herself in the bathtub. She handed off the baby and sank deep into her own territory—where she could rest her end zone for a while.

THE FLEX TEST

Another thing that affects the way we communicate with our husbands is how flexible they are in their opinions. I would even venture to say that, when it comes to the subject of where you work, your husband falls into one of two categories: flexible or inflexible.

Inflexible husbands are pretty easy to spot. They're the ones running around, saying things like: "This is the way things are going to be! I am in control here! I have spoken!" (They use a lot of exclamation marks when they speak.) The flexible ones are, well, everybody else.

I have a distinct advantage in discussing this subject because I've been married to one of each. My ex had no flex. His motto was, "My way or the highway!" Let me tell you, the highway never looked so good. Arnold, on the other hand, says, "Let's walk down this road together," and that's what we do. It's a personal bias, I know, but I prefer the latter.

Flexible husbands are pretty easy to deal with. Arnold listens to me when I need to talk about my feelings. I'm not sure he always understands what I'm talking about, but he does listen. When I have made career changes to or from the workplace, he supported me. We talked over the options, looked at the financial and emotional fallout, and came to a decision together. This method of working things out is very honoring to both of us, and very satisfying, too.

FATHER FACT:
According to the U.S. Census Bureau, men are now the primary caregivers in one out of every five dual-earner households with preschool children.

Flexible husbands can be like mine, assuming all or most of the financial responsibility for the family. They can also be like Mike, an acquaintance of mine who stays home with the kids while his wife pursues her fast-track career. "I work nights, at a minimum-wage job," he told me, "just to help make ends meet. Because of my wife's career, it makes more sense for her to work full-time. When the kids get to school age, I'll go back to school, too. Until then, this arrangement works out for our family."

But what do you do if you are married to one of those *other* guys, an inflexible husband? This man can be hard to talk to. He already has his mind made up about how things ought to be. One type of inflexible husband thinks he shouldn't have to shoulder all the financial responsibility alone, so he lays down the law: The wife shall work! End of subject! Discussion closed!

At the other end of the inflexible extreme, you may be dealing with a ''no wife of mine is going to work!'' kind of guy. Either way, if you're a mom facing such inflexible opinions, you have your communication work cut out for you. So what do you do? How do you talk to him about what *you* want?

One choice, although I can't say that I recommend it, is the path of least resistance. This time-honored strategy is practiced by millions of moms all over the world—because it works. The rules are simple: Keep the peace, and Don't rock the boat.

I know all about using the path of least resistance with an inflexible husband. I tried it once with my ex, and I have to tell you, it was kind of nice not having to make any decisions or take responsibility for anything. I just relaxed and he took over. I did whatever he said. The peace was kept. I can understand, firsthand, the appeal this strategy has when you live with an inflexible man.

Unfortunately (or fortunately, as it turned out), I had trouble keeping up the path of least resistance strategy for very long. I'm kind of ornery, and, after the novelty wore off, I got tired of always being told what to do. So naturally I opted for action at the opposite extreme: Do whatever you want regardless of what he thinks.

Now, this is a plan of action for the independent woman! Do your own thing! Hoe your own row! Always use exclamation points when you talk!

This strategy works well, as long as you don't mind raising the kids on your own (assuming you get custody of them in the divorce settlement).

HAND IN HAND

When discussing important subjects with your husband, try this little secret: Hold his hand. There's something about holding hands that smooths out what could otherwise be a heated exchange. Holding someone's hand is an act of kindness, and kindness begets kindness. It links the two of you together physically, which helps keep the communication link going, too. It's hard to be angry with someone who's holding your hand. When you're holding hands, you can't cross your arms over your chest and say "Humph!" (Well, maybe you could, but it would be awkward.) Reaching out and holding your husband's hand can also settle down a conversation that's getting *out* of hand. Try this at home! You don't have to be a professional to do it!

If you would like to find a way to respond to an inflexible husband that is somewhere between "roll over and play dead" and "stand up and fight!" there is another alternative.

It's one of those simple things—so simple that it either has to work, or it can't possibly. You sit down with him, look him in the eyes, take a deep breath . . . and tell him how you feel. He might even hear you—who knows? If you're not ready to talk to him face to face about your feelings about where you work, try writing him a letter. The important thing here is to open the door. Trust him enough to be waiting on the other side.

Of course, all this would be a lot easier if those men would just learn to listen to us!

SAY, WHAT?

Yes, we wish our husbands could develop better listening skills. Like us. We're great listeners! Especially when someone has something wonderfully juicy to tell us, then we're all ears. And we always consider everyone else's feelings before we make any major decisions. And we never do anything without thinking it through. Never!

Well, I have to admit that sometimes I get so wrapped up in what I want to do that I don't even notice what's going on with anyone else. Sometimes I'm so focused on trying to figure out what's going to work for *me* that I don't look at what's going to work for *us*. And then I have to stop complaining about how my husband doesn't listen to me and ask myself, How good am I at listening to my husband?

How good are you at listening to yours?

It's just a question. Think about it. I'm not pointing any fingers here. I have noticed, though, that when Arnold and I have really important things to talk about, the conversation goes along a lot more smoothly if I take the time to at least *try* to see things from his viewpoint. And that means I really have to listen to what he's saying. All the way through. To the end. It means that I have to care enough about him to keep my mouth closed while he finishes a sentence.

It's a tall order, I know. But it's amazing what you can endure when you love someone.

PICTURE THIS

Sometimes I like to indulge my imagination and think about how things would be in a perfect world. People would take responsibility for their own actions. Our kids' biggest worry would be studying for the next exam at a violence-free school. Men and women would work together with respect for each other. My husband would be able to read my mind—when it is convenient for me, of course.

Ah, but the best thing would be this—that men and women would marry to make a life together, a life in which they would honor each other with their actions, through thoughtfulness and kindness to each other.

At the very least, we ought to be able to talk to our husbands, and listen to what they have to say.

Get the picture?

CHAPTER 6 ∽

TOP TEN REASONS NOT TO QUIT YOUR DAY JOB

(To become a stay-at-home mom.)

The best plan is to profit by the folly of others.
—Pliny the Elder, circa a.d. 23–79

On guard!

We've been talking a lot about different aspects of working outside the home, and why it may or may not be a good choice for you. Maybe you've even identified a few reasons for quitting your job. After looking at some of those not-so-positive attributes to working, you might even be thinking that this staying home thing sounds pretty good.

Before you rush home and start baking cookies or something, I would ask that you be careful to make that choice based on the right reasons.

What are the wrong reasons?

I'm so glad you asked . . .

REASON TEN

Don't quit your day job to become a stay-at-home mom because Ed McMahon sent you a letter promising you $10 million (if you return the winning number).

Ed and me are buds. He writes to me *all the time*. But he has yet to send me anything other than a nice magazine now and then.

Don't you just hate it when that happens?

My husband and I recently went sailing off the coast of Santa Barbara, and our latest dream was born—to sail around the world. It's fun to dream about things like that, especially things like winning a lot of money. *Somebody* has to win, I tell myself. Might as well be me. But until Ed comes through with the cash, I'm holding off on the yacht order.

Don't quit your day job because you hope something wonderful and profitable will happen to you.

You can't bank on it if it ain't in the bank.

REASON NINE

Don't quit your day job to become a stay-at-home mom because you got first place in a karaoke contest.

You know me—I'm teasing again—just enough to make a point. You might be tempted to throw a good job away because a long-shot opportunity presents itself. You might even tell yourself you can do this great thing from home and spend more time with your kids. Before you do, though, make sure the bills are still going to be paid, and that you and the kids will still be able to eat.

REASON EIGHT

Don't quit your day job to become a stay-at-home mom because you embarrassed yourself at the company Christmas party (possibly during the karaoke contest).

Once, many moons ago, I started a new job at the end of the year. I was also in the throes of some stupid diet where I could eat about three calories a day as long as those calories had no carbohydrates in them. I showed up at the boss's house for the Christmas party on Friday night and decided that the only refreshment he was offering that fit into my diet was straight vodka.

Do I have to say it? Isn't it obvious? Would I be telling you about this incident here, at this particular time and place, if I hadn't thoroughly embarrassed myself?

Going to work on Monday morning was one of the hardest things I ever had to do in my life. It was so tempting just to fade away into the background and never be seen or heard from again. I imagined that people would think of me only with a passing interest. "Oh, her? Yes, wasn't she the one at the Christmas party. . . ?" people would ask. "Yes, yes, she's the one," others would answer, shaking their heads, tsk-tsking as they got back to their duties.

But I needed the job. I plucked up my courage, tucked my tail between my legs, went to work, and started apologizing. My coworkers were gracious enough to assure me that I hadn't behaved *that* badly, and the whole thing blew over. And it turned out to be one of the best jobs I ever had.

Moral of the story: If you do something stupid (or embarrassing), own up to it and get back to work. Life goes on whether or not you have a paycheck, and generally we mortify ourselves to a far greater degree than anyone else notices. (They're all worrying about the embarrassing things *they* did, anyway.)

REASON SEVEN

Don't quit your day job to become a stay-at-home mom because you miss daytime TV.

Erica got married again. I haven't seen *All My Children* in years but I watched it long enough to be certain that Erica's still walking down the aisle. I quit watching the show when I noticed that the only time the show introduced new male characters was when Erica had married and divorced everyone in the current cast. Maybe that's why Susan Lucci missed the Emmy all those years . . . people have a hard time feeling good about such a fickle character, even if she is fictional.

Life is more than television. Really. Trust me on this one. If you're thinking about quitting your day job, make sure your reason is something more than wanting to veg out in front of the tube. Quit because you want to offer *more* to the world, not because you want to offer less. Sometimes people just give up, check out, go into hibernation. If you want to leave your job, fine. But do it because you want to move toward something productive, not just to run away from something you don't like.

REASON SIX

Don't quit your day job to become a stay-at-home mom because you're mad at your husband.

"I'll show him!" Have you ever said that? And then you went off and did something you never would have done otherwise—just so you could "show" him. Or your mother-in-law. Or whomever.

Revenge is a very bad reason to quit your job. You're a responsible, intelligent adult. You want to make responsible, intelligent decisions—decisions that are good for you and that help you to accomplish your goals. You'll do just fine as long as you remember that your goals are to do what's best for you and for your family. When revenge becomes your goal, chances are you'll end up doing something that's not best for anybody.

If you doubt that, just check out some of the TV talk shows. Oh . . . never mind. They're on daytime TV.

Keep your goals in mind. Don't let momentary anger get you off track. You're better than that.

REASON FIVE

Don't quit your day job to become a stay-at-home mom because you're not getting along with a coworker.

Yes, yes, I know. That so-and-so is making your life miserable. You can hardly face getting up and going to work every morning because you're going to have to face *her* (or *him*). You just know everything would be perfect if *they* weren't around. Then you start thinking, maybe if *you* weren't around that job, your life would be happier because you wouldn't have to deal with *them*.

No one ever said you have to like everyone you work with, or that they have to like you. True, personalities of your coworkers can make a difference in how much enjoyment you get from your job. But running away from a job because of "those types of people" doesn't guarantee that you won't run into someone just like them on your way out. Even stay-at-home moms have to deal with people with difficult personalities. They're everywhere!

Before you quit your job because of difficult coworkers, try to see things from their perspective. Is it possible you are being difficult, too? You'll be better off if you try to work things out the best you can, and just get on with the job at hand.

REASON FOUR

Don't quit your day job to become a stay-at-home mom because you didn't get that raise you deserve.

Okay. This falls under the category of "do as I say, not as I do." Once upon a time (again, when I was young, and, shall we say, uh, less wise than I am today) I was working in a job making $7.25 per hour. Somehow I got a burr in my begonia that I deserved $7.50 per hour, and I told my employer as much. For reasons known only to him, he was not in agreement with my assessment of the situation and suggested I go water my begonia and get back to work.

Well! I showed him! I took my begonia and planted it in my flower bed at home!

Then I put my head in my hands and wailed, "Why on earth did I do that?"

In a complete panic, I rushed out and found another job making $8 an hour. In other words, I lucked out. It would have been just as easy, and I wouldn't have had to miss a paycheck or two, to find that new job before transplanting my begonia (if you know what I mean).

Be careful not to make rash decisions (as I did) based on emotion, before you know what your options are. Luck is a poor substitute for groceries.

REASON THREE

Don't quit your day job to become a stay-at-home mom because you work for a jerk.

Tell me about it. I've been there. Done that. But don't get me wrong. I think leaving a job, if you can, where you work for a jerk, is a good thing to do. Life is too short to put up with manipulating mini-moguls whose only goal in life (it seems) is to make your life miserable. (Actually, their true goals in life are to take care of their own interests—the fallout that lands on your working life is simply a function of whether your existence and input is convenient or inconvenient for them at any given moment.)

The trick here is to not make a life-changing decision to become a stay-at-home mom simply because you work for a jerk. Take Susan. She put up with working for a jerk for years. Couldn't make him happy. Worked all kinds of overtime. Got nowhere.

But Susan didn't fly out of the office half-cocked, vowing to leave the working world forever because of this jerk she worked for. No. She calmly evaluated her situation, realized that for her family's well-being she needed a job—but she didn't need this particular job! So she got another one.

"It's been so nice," she told me, "to be relaxed about my work. My husband commented that I had been mad for all the years I worked at the other place, and he was glad I changed. The kids got their mom back."

So think about it. Maybe you don't need to come home. Maybe the best thing you can do for your family is to get another job. Don't let working for a jerk cloud your good judgment.

REASON TWO

Don't quit your day job to become a stay-at-home mom because your next-door neighbor (cousin, sister, coworker) did it.

I can hear my mother now. "If your friends all jumped off a cliff, would you do it, too?"

I probably answered, "Well, it depends."

Doing something just because it seems like everyone else is doing it can be very bad news. For moms looking at the whole working issue, this rule can work both ways. It's not a good idea for a stay-at-home mom to get a job just because it seems like all the other mothers are working, and it's not a good idea for a working mom to go home just because it may seem like more women are staying home nowadays.

Sometimes we're tempted to go along with the crowd because we want to be accepted. We say to ourselves, "She seems happy—maybe that would work for me." That's fine, for a beginning. But we need to remember to make choices based on the circumstances of our own lives, not anybody else's.

REASON ONE

Don't quit your day job to become a stay-at-home mom because your mother (husband, friend, analyst) thinks you should.

I can't stand it when people can't make up their own minds. It's like they have to check out everything they do with someone else first to make sure it's okay. Never had an independent thought in their lives. Why, I wish people like that would just . . . wait a minute . . .

Wasn't there a time in my life when I wouldn't even go to the mall unless one of my friends went with me?

And didn't I major in accounting (instead of English—like I wanted to) because my mother thought I should train for a career where I could actually make money?

Yes, I have been known to make major life changes because I thought it would make someone else happy, without much regard to whether it was something I really wanted to do. But, I'm here to tell you, it doesn't work. Not by a long shot.

Sometimes I get nervous about telling people what to do, or in the case of this top-ten list, what not to do. You may realize, by now, that the resource I used for compiling this list is my own life. I want you to benefit from my experience. Somehow, it would give meaning to all those stupid things I've done in the past if someone else could be saved from making the same mistakes.

Whatever reasons you use in making your life choices, make sure they are *your* reasons. And please, until you've sorted out what your reasons are, don't quit your day job.

Okay?

CHAPTER 7 ∽

PINK SLIP BLUES

(A Guide for the Downsized and Out.)

Everything has an end.

—AFRICAN SAYING

THE "NO CHOICE" CHOICE

Well, how's your evaluation of your life going? Does working work for you? Maybe you've looked at the money end of it, and found you do make enough, even after taxes and other expenses, to justify spending most of your waking hours at a job. Perhaps you've discovered that working meets your survival or self-esteem needs. Your kids seem to be doing okay. You do a fair to above average job of juggling all those different responsibilities. Maybe you have even strengthened your resolve to be in control of your own life and your own choices. In fact, it's entirely possible you have decided that working outside the home fits your life quite well!

But there's one other aspect of this whole choice issue that we haven't looked at yet. Call it the "no choice" choice. It happens when, in spite of everything you've examined and figured out, and regardless of the choices you've made for yourself, someone else makes your working choice for you. It can happen when staying home is the furthest thing from your mind. It does happen when you hear those dreaded words . . .

"You Don't Work Here Anymore"

Anne made her usual stop at the break room on the way to her cubicle. It was Friday morning. As she fished in her wallet for some change, her friend Paula walked in through the break room door.

"Did you hear the news this morning?" Paula asked.

"Yeah," Anne said, "I heard it on the car radio. They said Valco was going to lay off ten percent of the employees today. Do you think it will really happen?"

"I don't know. All I know is that something has to give—and soon. Everybody is so jumpy!" Paula poured herself a cup of hot coffee and grabbed a packet of artificial sweetener. The fresh coffee aroma filled the tiny room. "I've never seen it this bad before."

"I don't even want to go to my desk," said Anne. "There are ten people in my department, and I've been there the shortest time. If one of us goes, it'll probably be me."

"What would you do if you got laid off?"

Anne pushed the "diet" button on the soda machine. The can rattled down with a familiar *clump*.

"I don't know." She sighed as she popped open the can. "Sometimes I think this is not such a great job. But I don't want to—you know—get fired. What if I couldn't find another job? We just bought a new house!"

"I know what you mean," said Paula. "I'm paying for Jody's braces with the company dental plan. I wonder what happens to stuff like that?"

Wrapping a napkin around the cold soft drink can, Anne

turned toward the door. "We'd better get to work," she said. "Good luck. Call me if anything happens."

"Sure. You, too."

Anne made her way over to the little cubicle she had called home for the last three years. A piece of paper sat on her desk. Right in the middle. Where she would be sure to see it. First thing.

She picked it up. The muscles in her chest tightened. "Please see me as soon as you get in," the note said. It was signed Bill. Her manager.

This is it, she thought. She took a deep breath, then walked down the hall toward the manager's office.

By the time Anne got back to her cubicle she was numb. She tried to hold back the tears, but they splashed down anyway into the box Bill had given her so she could pack her things. The empty box blurred as she put it on the floor. She sat down. This little space wasn't hers anymore. Bill didn't even want her to finish out the day.

I've lost my job, she thought. *What am I going to do?* She thought about their new house and the mortgage they couldn't handle on Steve's salary alone. She thought about how she had promised Danny he could have his birthday party at the amusement park next month. But now—how could they afford it? How could they possibly keep up Lisa's piano lessons? She thought about how happy her husband had been when she got this job. *What am I going to tell Steve?*

"Due to no fault of your own," Bill had said—right before he told her he was sorry. Someone higher up had made the decision. Knowing that didn't help much—she was still the one out of a job. Anne reached for a tissue and blew her nose. She had to get hold of herself. She had to pack her things in this stupid box.

It was time to go home.

FEAR—THE REAL "F" WORD

I hope you never have to endure the pain and fear of losing a job. But chances are, you or someone close to you will. Such are the times in which we live. I can't think of one person I know who hasn't been affected in some way by layoffs somewhere. It's scary. Having a job today means you have a job—today. Who knows about tomorrow?

Gone are the days when the norm was staying with one job or one company until you qualified for a gold watch and a retirement party. We've said goodbye to job security and hello to "Hey—you're lucky if you even have a job!" A mother can choose from now until the kids leave home that working outside the home is for her, and it won't do her a bit of good if she can't find a job or count on keeping the one she has. Puts a whole new slant on the choice issue, doesn't it?

I mean, it's one thing to examine your life and decide you want to be a stay-at-home mom. It's something else altogether to have someone else announce that "through no fault of your own, your services are no longer required." I know. I've been there.

Allow me to share my credentials here. Ahem. I consider myself an expert in this area because Anne, whom you previously met, is just like me. Actually, she is me! Her story is, basically, my story. Besides that, my husband and I have also lived through his job disintegrating. He and I have done a lot of hands-on research on the subject of being laid off. We've both experienced the fear, panic, and uncertainty of suddenly losing half or all of the family's income. We know what losing a job feels like, and believe me, it doesn't feel good.

But is it the end of the world?

No.

It may seem like the end of the world, however, if it happens to you! It's like the difference between knowing someone who broke her leg and having a broken leg yourself. "Oh, yes. Mary had a nasty fall skiing and broke her leg. I hear that fourteen percent of skiers break bones each season." But when it's *your* fall and *your* broken leg, the story takes on a more urgent tone. "I thought I was going to die! I was going way too fast and then the slope just disappeared out from under me! After I fell, I didn't know if I would ever get up again!"

We could have a really nice, clinical discussion here on, say, Ten Things to Do If You Lose Your Job, and it might even help a little. But if your job disappears out from under you and you find yourself face to face with the fear that follows the fall—trust me, you won't be feeling very clinical. You'll be scared out of your wits.

So let's start with the fear and see if we can't get past it. You may want to ski again someday—or get another job—who knows? But, hey. I'm here for you.

ON THE INSIDE LOOKING OUT?

Maybe you're one of the lucky ones, and you won't have to go through the painful process of losing a job. But you might have asked yourself, "What can I do for my friend when it happens to her?"

It's so hard to know what to do, or what to say, when someone we care about is experiencing difficult times in her life. Keep reading this chapter! You'll understand better what she is experiencing. And watch the sidebars for ways you can really help a friend who has lost a job.

FIRST, YOU CRY

Here's the good news. It's okay to cry. As a matter of fact, I'm pretty sure it's required. There's a list (isn't there?) of life events when you're supposed to cry: when someone gets married, when someone dies, when your children are born, when your in-laws move in. Losing a job must be on that list somewhere!

So go ahead and cry. You're entitled to a little panic attack now and then. Throw yourself a real pity party. Woe-woe-woe to your heart's content. Sit like a lump on the sofa and collect fuzz from your navel. Disappear under the bedspread until you become one with the mattress.

> **SILENCE IS GOLDEN . . .**
>
> Give your friend some time to grieve over the lost job. Go ahead and call her—let her cry on your shoulder— but hold back on any advice you may want to share. For a little while, anyway.

After a decent interval of self-indulgence, take a break. (You'll need it, and so will the people who live with you.)

GO WITH THE FLOW

When you come up for air, take a look at the following flow chart. Think of it as a road map to your new life. Now, if you got a chart like this from the government, it would probably be entitled something like "Guide to Nonvoluntary Post-Employment Choices." But, fortunately, this is just you and me here. We'll just call the chart, "Job's Gone—Now What?"

The first thing you'll notice about the flow chart is that crying, moaning, and all that other good stuff is listed there for you (just in case you've forgotten how to panic). Feel free to stay in the panic loop for a while. But be careful not to stay there too long—you might wear a hole in the sofa.

COUNT YOUR BLESSINGS

Okay. When you've cried through all the tissue in the house, it's time to move on to the next step of the chart: Count your

Job's Gone—Now What?

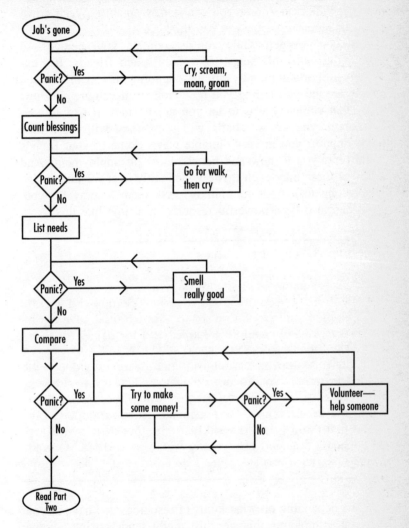

blessings. Drag yourself over to a table. Sit down. Get out a piece of paper (no kidding) and write down all the things you have going for you. Do you have a husband? Does he still have a job? Are you eligible to collect unemployment compensation?

Do you have any savings? Maybe there are some life insurance policies with cash values you can borrow against. Write down every financial resource you can think of.

And don't forget, while you're counting your pennies, to count your other blessings: your family and friends. It's extremely important to rally all the support you can. You need people around you telling you how wonderful you are and how crazy that company was to let you go. Besides, if people who care about you know what's going on, they will more than likely support you in very tangible ways. Some of your friends could refer you to new and better places of employment! And a few of them may even invite your family over for dinner. Do you belong to a faith community? Ask them to pray for you. Faith can also be a powerful resource at a time like this.

DID YOU CATCH THAT CUE?

Okay, family and friends! If you're paying attention, you've noticed that I gave your unemployed friend something to look forward to—from you! So give her a call. Invite her and the family over for dinner, or take her a casserole and a salad.

While you're at it, offer to share a rented video with her family. (You're not going to watch it for *all* three days, are you?) Or better yet, watch the video all together at your house and make an informal party out of it. Your friend doesn't have the money to spend on going out, and an evening with you and yours could give her a real lift!

Now, depending on what kinds of resources you have at your disposal, completing this step just might send you into another panic loop. That's the way it was for us when Arnold lost his job last year—not long after I had, after careful and painstaking evaluation, decided that the family could afford for me to stay home. Our income, which had already been cut in half by my choice, went to zero overnight. In addition, we had just bought a house and had stretched ourselves financially to the limit to swing the deal. The outlook was pretty bleak.

Even though we had many intangible blessings, including faith, friends, and family, we still needed to panic again. Just a little. But instead of crying and screaming and moaning, we hit the streets—and started walking. While we walked, we talked through our feelings. There was something about being out of the house (i.e., reminder of mortgage responsibility), and getting some fresh air and exercise, that helped us make it through. Sometimes we walked to a nearby park, and played on the swings like a couple of kids. And even though that was a very scary time, we have some happy memories of those walks together.

So consider this panic strategy: When you feel like crying, go for a walk. If the tears come anyway, maybe you can pretend it's just a nice little stroll in the rain. Do you feel like lumping it on the sofa? Walk to the park and play on the swings. If screaming seems appropriate, tell yourself you'll scream a lit-tle—right after a quick walk around the block.

HELLO, MASLOW

Between laps around the neighborhood, take a moment or two to move on down the flow chart to the next step: List your needs. Now it's time to get out a piece of paper and write down all your bills. ALL of them. There will be more than you ever dreamed possible.

This might be a good time to flip back and re-read Chapter Two. Maslow and his little hierarchy could take on a whole new perspective. Then look again at your list of bills. Are there any items that you could realistically omit from your budget? Maybe you'll find you could easily live without some things that seemed essential just the other day! It's amazing how many opportunities to save present themselves when cutting back is no longer an option.

In our case, eating out became a little luxury we simply could not afford. Fortunately, because of a pretty good backlog in the freezer, eating itself was still okay. We did have a few "surprise" casseroles, though. "What's that?" Ryan would ask. I would calmly and lovingly respond, "I don't know. I found it in the freezer. Just eat it and be grateful you have food on your plate!" (It's nice to know that one can find adventure, even in the midst of adversity.)

DID I FORGET TO MENTION . . . ?

"Call me if you need anything" is a statement heard by people going through difficult times. I've said it myself, to my friends, and I meant it!

But I discovered during my own difficult time that the last thing I wanted to do was to call my friends and admit that I needed help. I was so grateful when one of them would call *me*, or just show up on my front doorstep with dinner.

If you really want to help your friend, don't wait for her to call you. Offer some of the things we talked about earlier, or offer to watch her kids, or anything you can think of that might smooth her path a little. Maybe she just needs someone to talk to, but she doesn't want to "bother" anyone with her problems. Just give her a call and ask her how she's doing.

But don't wait for her to call you!

Be forewarned, identifying an overabundance of financial needs may result in another visit to the panic loop. If so, when you get back from your walk, take a bubble bath. Use liquid dish soap if that's all you have. Put a little cologne in the bathwater. It's hard to feel too depressed when you smell really good.

TIME IS ON YOUR SIDE

The next step is strictly a math function. If you have trouble with math, use your fingers—preferably while the pleasant aroma from that comforting soak in the tub still clings to them. (It might soften the blow.) Are you ready? Okay. Compare your blessings with your bills. How long can you survive without finding another job?

This little exercise is going to tell you one of two things: Either you need to find another source of income right away, or you don't.

Maybe you've gone through all these steps and decided that you really must find another job—immediately. It's very difficult to look for a job after losing one, because the old self-esteem level can be pretty low. But, if you've been walking through your panics (as I so wisely suggested), you have probably lost a couple of pounds and are feeling more energetic.

Use that energy to update your résumé, make appointments for interviews, and clip grocery coupons. Between interviews, or while you're waiting for the "call-back," walk over to the library and check out a couple of books you've always wanted to read. Take advantage of having some time to yourself. Do some of the things you've always wanted to do around the house, but didn't have time for. You've been just dying to clean out that front closet—right?

THROUGH THE GRAPEVINE

Keep your eyes and ears open for job opportunities for your friend. Tell people you know about her, and what kinds of skills she has. You never know when you're going to run into someone who knows someone who is looking for someone just like her!

Even if nothing comes of it, your friend will appreciate having someone on her side.

I know—there are lulls in the search for a new job. And those lulls can wreak havoc with your confidence level. I'm certain that by now you're catching on to new and productive ways to panic. So when you find yourself in one of those lulls and feel that panicky feeling coming on, skip the moaning altogether. Do something positive instead, and this time, try doing something for someone else. Volunteer to work at your child's school, driving for field trips or helping out in the classroom. It feels great to be productive, plus you are able to focus on something other than *yourself* and *your problems*. This strategy benefits both you and others—what could be better than that?

PART-TIME IN NO TIME

Even if you find you need another full-time job right away, don't overlook working in part-time or temporary jobs in the interim. Temporary work can stretch out the financial safety net, giving you some much-needed breathing room to evaluate your options in full. Make use of your marketable skills by signing up with a temp service immediately.

The main thing to remember at this point is: *Keep busy! Keep walking!* And make sure you smell really good.

IN THE PINK

I love happy endings, don't you? It really is possible to survive the "no choice" choice with your health and dignity intact.

I suppose, to be completely fair, I'd have to say that it is also possible not to survive. I mean, you could get run over by a truck or something. However, I choose to concentrate on those things over which I have control. (And anyway, didn't I tell you this book isn't for everyone?)

Of course, there is one more step of the flow chart left to explore. It's that whole "staying home" thing. Maybe you discovered, when you compared your blessings with your bills, that the money just might last for a little while. Or maybe you're beginning to see that with just a few minor changes on your part, the family could survive on one income. If so, the door to the stay-at-home option just creaked open a bit.

When that door creaked open for me I ran through it, full force. I was disenchanted with the working world. My son needed more from me than I was giving. I was ready, willing, and able to come home, and I knew that the best was yet to come.

PART TWO

Coming Home

A man travels the world over
in search of what he needs
and returns home to find it.
—GEORGE MOORE, 1916

CHAPTER 8

GREAT EXPECTATIONS

By and large, mothers and housewives are the only workers who do not have regular time off. They are the great vacationless class.
—ANNE MORROW LINDBERGH, 1955

STRIKING OUT ON MY NEW ADVENTURE

The idea of coming home, of quitting my day job, filled me with wonder and delight. I just knew that everything was going to be perfect—now. My imagination teemed with elaborate visions of a carefree, unencumbered-by-a-job life. And I'm almost certain I heard violin music (and possibly even a harp) in the background, accompanying thoughts of my new and wonderful world. . .

THE PERFECT KIDS

I was certain that when I told my son I was coming home to be a stay-at-home mom he would perk right up and quit having any problems whatsoever. After all, if he was suffering

87

because he didn't have enough of my time, giving him my time would fix things. Isn't that how it's supposed to work? Identify problem. Identify solution. Execute solution. Problem goes away.

My fantasy went something like this:

> ME: Ryan, honey, I'm going to quit my job.
> RYAN: Really, Mom? How come?
> ME: Because I want to spend more time with you. You are very important to me!
> RYAN: Wow! That makes me feel great, Mom! Can I go clean my room now?
> ME: Why, of course! And when you're finished we'll bake some cookies together!
> RYAN: Cool! I can't wait! I love you, Mom! (Beaming.)
> ME: I love you, too, Ryan. (Gives son a motherly hug—tears of joy well in eyes.)

Yes, I could see it all. Mom comes home and son sprouts angelic wings and halo. My life would no longer be complicated by the demands of an outside job—I could focus all my love and attention on my precious child, who would show his gratitude to me by immediately turning into the model son I knew he must be inside.

REALITY STRIKES

Why doesn't reality ever cooperate with the way things ought to be? My actual conversation with Ryan went more like this:

> ME: Ryan, honey, I'm going to quit my job.
> RYAN: Oh. (Doesn't look up from comic book.) Do I still get to go to day care?
> ME: No, you'll be at home with me. I want to spend more time with you. You are very important to me.

RYAN: (Drops comic book.) What? Are you crazy?

ME: What do you mean by that?

RYAN: Mom, I have a lot of fun at day care. (Whining.) If I'm spending all my time with you I won't get to play with my friends!

ME: But we'll get to do things *together*. We can bake cookies!

RYAN: That's *girl* stuff! (Rolls eyes.) Are we done talking? Can I go play video games?

ME: Have you cleaned your room?

RYAN: Aw, Mom, you never let me have *any* fun! (Stomps off and slams bedroom door.)

Well, what do you know—my son didn't react the way I wanted him to! I wanted him to jump up and thank me for making the "sacrifice of coming home." I wanted him to tell me that I was the best mom in the world. I wanted to feel good about my decision and my new role in life. I wanted to bake cookies.

The mistake I made was in not trying to see my decision from his perspective. I was asking him to change his life—rather drastically. Heck, I didn't even ask him, I just told him how it was going to be! No wonder he didn't jump up and down with joy and jubilation. He was accustomed to things the way they were, and for most people "accustomed" means "comfortable." Ryan didn't react to having an at-home mom; he reacted to having his routine upset.

I didn't consider that he would need some time to adjust to the idea of having Mom around most of the time. He wasn't sure he liked the idea. During my first year at home I took him to school every day, volunteered in his classroom and in the school office, helped him with his homework, drove him to piano lessons, cheered him on at Cub Scout T-ball games, took special trips with him in the summer to visit family. These were all things I hadn't had time for before, when I was working. It was a rough year as we made many false starts into establishing new routines.

But toward the end of that year something wonderful happened—Ryan started talking to me. I mean, *really* talking—not the mindless babble that so easily issues from the mouth of an eight-year-old, but real, honest-to-goodness communication. He opened up like a flower on a spring day, telling me all his fears and hopes and dreams. He even told me about things that had bothered him way back before the time I came home. And that's when the healing—for both of us—began.

Today I wouldn't trade my time with him for anything. We reconnected, as parent and child. My coming home made a difference in him, a difference that other people have noticed and mentioned to me. But it didn't happen overnight, and every day isn't wonderful. I *can* tell you, though, that when I suggest baking cookies these days, he answers, "Cool, Mom!" (We're still working on the clean room concept. These things take time. I've been personally working on the concept for most of my life!)

THE PERFECT HOUSE

Another fantasy I entertained about coming home was what I consider the clean house myth. It goes something like this:

> When I'm a full-time stay-at-home mom, I'll have all kinds of time to do all the things I want to do; what's more, because I have all this time, my house will always be immaculate.
>
> I shall always be ready for unexpected guests, who will happily join me in my cozy world of stay-at-homeness. I will offer my guests flavored international coffees (their choice) served in coffee cups of a design appropriate to the season of the year. If perchance these guests should need a night's lodging, they will find a comfortable guest room with fresh linens, lilacs on the nightstand, and a chocolate on the pillow.

I shall be so successful at running my household that Martha Stewart will phone me for tips—which I shall graciously share. Dust, clutter, and disorganization will become a thing of the distant past, forgotten like a shadow of some bygone era.

When my family comes home at the end of the day, they will joyfully enter the cocoon of safe haven that I have created for their pleasure and benefit, and they will thank me for my efforts sincerely and often. I shall bask in the glow of their loving appreciation, curled up on the sofa in front of a crackling fire, enjoying my leisure time by reading and perhaps, on occasion, creating cross-stitch masterpieces that exhibit my singular good taste and decorum.

My husband will so appreciate the comfortable and relaxed atmosphere that I have painstakingly and tenderly created, that he will send the children to bed early so he can thank me properly.

Ah, yes. I shall enjoy a good stay-at-home life in my clean house!

REALITY STRIKES AGAIN

Are you one of those people whose house is always clean and organized? Don't talk to me. No—wait—on second thought, I do want you to talk to me. Tell me how you do it! Then leave me alone. People like you make people like me look bad.

I probably don't even need to tell you that my clean house fantasy was a tad off the mark. And I guess it's slightly possible that I got a little carried away. When constructing my fantasy, I forgot one thing: I hate to clean house! I'd rather write, or visit a friend in the hospital, or maybe even go to the hospital and schedule some elective surgery—anything so I won't have to clean house!

All kidding aside, I have more trouble keeping up with the household chores now that I'm home than I did when I was gone all day. For one thing, I make more messes with all my stay-at-home projects—like cooking dinner. And now that we're on the subject, if I'm the one who has to figure out what we're going to eat, and shop for the food, and bring it home from the store and put it away, and cook it, and serve it, why can't someone else do the dishes?

The real problem with the clean house myth is those *other* people who believe it. Take your husband, for example. He might be the kind of husband who thinks keeping the house clean is part of the "deal" that goes along with having a stay-at-home wife. Maybe if you don't deliver slippers and a pipe when he arrives home from work he'll start telling you that you're not living up to your part of the bargain. This whole clean house issue can be a real troublemaker.

The reality of the clean house myth is that some of us (or, rather, some of *you*) are naturally neat and tidy while the rest of us adhere to the old adage: "I prefer for my home to have a comfortable, lived-in look." You can tell who we are because if you drop in unexpectedly we'll open the front door only a crack so you can't see how comfortable and lived-in our house really looks! And if things get too "comfortable" for even our relaxed tastes, we'll plan a party or invite someone to dinner just so we'll *have* to clean the house.

For the rest of you neatniks, I need to say something: There *are* more important things than having a place for everything and everything in its place. Don't get me wrong. I enjoy a clean house as much as the next person. But don't let having one distract you from things like attending your kids' school programs, or noticing how great they're doing in math, or commenting on how kind and generous they are to other people. They need recognition from you for the things they do right. Try to point out some of those before you quite justifiably remind them they left a wet towel on the bathroom floor.

If this clean house thing is going to be a big issue for your family, and if housework is not on your Top Ten List of Things I'd Do Even If No One Paid Me (and trust me, no one will), you might be better off staying in your outside job (or getting one) and hiring a maid. Another choice is to stay home anyway and take some classes such as Your Friend the Toilet Brush or House Cleaning for the Neatness-Impaired Individual. If you can afford it, of course, stay home anyway and hire a maid.

I really hope you're the naturally neat and tidy type. If you're not, make sure you have room on your social calendar for at least one dinner party each month. That'll keep things livable.

THE PERFECT LIFE

I think working mothers entertain the fantasy that once we come home, we will be in total control of our time. Flexibility is, after all, touted as one of the benefits of being a stay-at-home mom. We like the idea of calling the shots, of not being forced to fit family life around the dictates of a job.

I envisioned lunch dates with friends and grocery shopping on a weekday morning (pure heaven for a person who likes to ramble through a nearly empty store instead of fighting her way down an aisle filled with other people and their shopping carts). I really did think I was going to have time to keep the house clean, and garden, and take the dogs for walks, and finally get in shape, and cook healthy and elaborate meals, and volunteer at school, and help Ryan with his homework, and learn French, and repaint the house, and write, and serve on the women's board at my church, and produce a school newsletter. And in my spare time I was going to organize the junk drawer and keep the kitchen table clear of miscellaneous papers and unsolicited mail. With the pressing time demands of my job removed, I just knew I would have time for all this and much, much more, once I came home.

All I had ever needed was time and the opportunity to do all these wonderful things! At least that's what I thought.

STRIKE THREE—YOU'RE OUT!

I'm sure you've figured out what happened to this fantasy. But since I'm the one telling this story, I'll say it anyway. Or maybe Gail, a mom in Arizona, puts it best:

"Let me tell you that you don't have any more time to do the things you want to do for yourself if you are at home than you do if you work. The only thing you can do in either case to make the time for the things that are really important to you."

Well said, well said. But why don't we have any more time than before? What takes up our time?

Let's see—there's the kids, the reason many of us choose to stay home in the first place. Remember—*you* are now doing the job that you paid your day care provider to do! Kids take a ton of time—and attention. Which reminds me, working mothers don't have the corner on guilt! Stay-at-home moms struggle with guilt, too. There's always some project or other we feel we ought to be working on (like laundry—I mean, do you want clean underwear or not?), and it's often difficult to take care of those things and pay attention to the kids at the same time. At least it is for a one-thing-at-a-time person like me. And if we give the kidlets the attention we think they need, and let the house go, we have to hope dear old dad will understand when he comes home, and not start asking questions like "What *did* you do all day?"

Another time-taker is your friend Gabriella. You know, the one you call Gabby for short. She likes to phone to check in with you just to see how you're doing, and forty-five minutes later you finally get a chance to tell her you just got out of the shower and you're afraid you might get electrocuted if you continue to hold the phone while standing in that puddle of water. By the way, I recommend investing in a cordless phone. That way you can keep moving (and working) when Gabby calls.

Then there are the errands—all the little places you have to go to drop off and pick up people and things. And the house-cleaning. And the doctor and dentist appointments for the kids.

And the laundry (yes, I know I already mentioned it, but I believe any chore that never gets done deserves extra weight). And the school conferences. And the school programs. And the listening to your kids. And the talking to your kids. And all those things you volunteer for because you have so much time. And the menu planning. And the grocery shopping. And the cooking. And driving the kids to school. And picking them up. And taking them to music lessons. And picking them up. And teaching them what they need to know about life. And taking them to soccer practice. And picking them up. And taking them to scouts. And picking them up. And taking them to their friend's house to play. And picking them up. And showing them how to tie their shoes. And how to ride a bicycle without falling. And picking them up. And. . .wait a minute! All this sounds like work!

Oh, yeah. *All mothers work*. I almost forgot!

CHAPTER 9 ∽

IDENTITY CRISIS

(No mom is an island.)

*No one can make you feel inferior without
your consent.*
— Eleanor Roosevelt, 1937

"Hi, i used to be a . . ."

I'm convinced that one of the biggest fears mothers have
about coming home is that we will lose our identities. We are
afraid of being "somebody's wife," or "somebody's mother,"
when what we want is to be *somebody*.

At a job it is easy. Who you are is what you do. You have
a job description that tells you what to do. You're accountable
to someone who makes sure you are doing what you are supposed to be doing. You get feedback and reinforcement as to
how you're doing. You get paid for what you do.

But at home, it's not so easy. Who you are is still what you
do, but you don't always know what to do! There are no job
descriptions, no paychecks, no merit increases. What's more,
coming home means letting go of what you used to do, and to
a great extent, what you used to be. And that can be difficult.

I'm reminded of that truth whenever I meet someone new. Even though I love being at home and am living out my lifelong dream of writing for a living, I almost always let it slip into the conversation that I have a degree in accounting. I identified myself as an accountant for so long, it seems I still have the need to let people know about that part of me. It isn't easy to let go of all the years I invested into that "accountant person."

Coming home, for a mother who's been in the workforce for any length of time, can be a big challenge. It can feel like a huge step backward, because you're leaving a portion of who you are behind—on purpose! And that can be very scary. You feel like you're. . .

Starting Over

Claire's eyes had barely closed when the baby started crying again. She groaned and pulled herself up off the bed, every bone and muscle in her body begging for sleep. She thought the baby would doze right off after eating his lunch, but ten-week-old Jeremy simply wasn't cooperating with her today.

"Oh, sweety," she said wearily as she reached into Jeremy's crib. His tiny face, scrunched up from crying, smoothed as she gently stroked his cheek. "Aren't you going to get any sleep today?" Still stroking his cheek, she moved her other hand around the crib mattress until she found the pacifier. Claire plugged it back into the baby's mouth, and soft sucking sounds replaced his cries. She stood next to the crib until his eyes closed, then tiptoed out of the nursery.

Yawning, Claire headed for the den. She knew she better sleep while the sleeping was good—namely, while Jeremy was down. But now, because she had trained herself to keep going even if her body knew better, she was awake again.

Claire plopped onto the sofa and eyed the TV. She

folded her arms in defiance. "No, I'm not going to pick up the remote," she said out loud. She couldn't even see the remote. Her gaze took in the once tidy room, now strewn with baby toys and dirty dishes. *The house never looked this bad before,* she thought. *Whatever made me think I wanted to stay home full-time?*

A familiar tightness gripped her chest as she thought again about leaving her job and her friends. Diane and Leslie were having lunch without her these days, and Claire wondered, *Do they miss me?* Her coworkers had visited her in the hospital right after Jeremy was born, but she hadn't seen them since. The few times they had talked on the phone felt strained, as if suddenly the only thing they had in common was the fact that they used to work together.

"Everything's changed," Claire said out loud. She had noticed that she was talking to herself a lot these days. But what else was there to do? All she did anymore was take care of Jeremy and watch the house get messier. With a sigh, Claire stretched out on the sofa and tried to position her head on the padded armrest. She reached down to pick up a throw pillow that had fallen onto the floor. There, on the floor where the pillow had been, was the remote control.

She didn't know she had picked the thing up. She only knew that she was pushing buttons, and suddenly, thankfully, there were voices coming into her world other than her own.

LOST, LONELY, AND GOING CRAZY

I've heard it a million times. Okay, maybe not a million. Sometimes I exaggerate. Let's say I've heard it many, many times. You've heard it, too. "If I was at home, I'd go crazy!" Or maybe you've heard a variation on the theme: "I stayed home for a while, but I was going crazy, so I went back to work.''

Claire is starting to go a little crazy. She misses her work friends. Staying home isn't as much fun as she thought it would be. She feels lost. She doesn't know what to *do* with herself. She doesn't know who she is anymore.

It happens to the best of us. We come home with the noblest intentions, but we get hung up somewhere along the way. Maybe we don't want to let go of what we used to do, or maybe we do let go, but we don't know exactly what to put in its place. So we end up like Claire, feeling lost and alone, stretched out in front of the TV.

I believe that those of us who ''go crazy'' at home do it to ourselves. I did it. As a matter of fact, I was quite accomplished at the going-crazy part of staying home. It's really very easy to do. You just, basically, do nothing. Except take care of everyone else in the family, of course. Oh, and you need to put in a fair amount of time feeling sorry for yourself. Just follow those elementary steps, and I guarantee, you'll go crazy every time.

I discovered, however, that I didn't have to settle for ''going crazy'' at home. I had choices. As a matter of fact, I realized that we moms have a built-in defense system for these types of situations. We're lucky that way!

When we're lost, we ask for directions.

FINDING YOUR WAY

The best way I know to find out how to create a new identity as a successful stay-at-home mom is to find a successful stay-at-home mom and make her tell you everything she knows. Follow her around. Feed her if you have to. Just don't give up until she spills her guts. What does she do all day? Is she happy? How does she make staying home work for her? I've talked to a number of these moms, and the happiest and most successful ones all seem to have one very important thing in common.

They don't really stay home.

What? Stay-at-home moms who don't stay home? Isn't that against the law or something? Doesn't "stay at home" mean "totally devote yourself to the well-being of every person on earth other than yourself and never exit the confines of your own house (except to go to the grocery store)"?

Of course it doesn't. If you want to be a happy, healthy, successful mom at home, I'm here to tell you that "stay at home" really means "get out of the house".

Years ago, I was discussing child rearing with a friend. "I can tell when I've been spending too much time with the kids," she told me.

"Oh, really? How's that?" I asked.

"It's easy," she said. "When my husband comes home in the evening and I ask him if he needs to go potty, that's my cue to get out more."

My friend was definitely on to something. To become a happy, healthy, successful stay-at-home mom, you need to get involved in something other than taking care of the kids and the traditional household duties. Please don't misunderstand. Kid care and house maintenance are important. Usually, the reason we want to come home in the first place is to have more time for the domestic end of our existence. But who are we kidding? There's more to life than sorting socks.

I guess the next logical question is, if we're supposed to get out of the house to be successful stay-at-home moms, just where the heck are we supposed to go—especially since we're now unemployed and don't have any money to do anything? Well, I can offer you some hope, but be aware—this is one of those things you have to figure out for yourself. Hey, you don't expect me to do *all* the work, do you?

I'm not totally heartless, though. I *can* give you some directions. What we're after here, as usual, is balance. Think about your car's engine for a minute. Whether or not you are mechanically inclined, you probably understand that the engine needs oil. Otherwise that little red "engine" light comes on in your dashboard and bad things happen involving smoke, tow trucks, and big repair bills. Don't ask me how I know this—I just do.

You see, a successful stay-at-home mom is to her family as oil is to an engine. She doesn't get all the glory, but without her, the family would come to a grinding halt. And in the same way that oil needs to be changed periodically, she needs to be refreshed from time to time.

What do you find refreshing? If you have preschoolers at home, you might find a baby-sitting co-op very refreshing. That

---

"VIRTUAL" FRIENDSHIPS

I realize that there might be a few moms who really *can't* get out of the house, even though you desperately want to. Thanks to the computer age, and on-line services, there's hope for you, too.

If you own a computer, consider signing up with an on-line service such as Prodigy, America Online, or CompuServe. Each of these services has special areas for moms to get together and talk about raising kids, or anything else for that matter. You can "chat" with these new friends simply by typing a message on your computer—your friends read your message wherever they are and type back. Right away! Just watch how much time you spend in this activity. If you're not careful, it can be very expensive.

The on-line services also offer "bulletin boards" where you can post a message that can be read by anyone who stops by—just like a real bulletin board. It's a little bit slower way of communication, but much more economical than chatting, and friendships have also started in these areas.

If you want, you can even find an e-mail (electronic mail) penpal to correspond with. It's a great way to find support and feel connected with the world.

way you can acquire some time away from home while leaving your children with a trusted friend—with no cash outlay! You might want to play tennis during this time, take a photography class, or attend a moms' group meeting. Maybe you'd like to volunteer some time at the local blood bank, or serve lunch at a homeless shelter.

Are your kids in school? Spend one afternoon a week as a teacher's aide. I enjoy picking up my son's classmates after school and taking them where they need to be. Their moms reimburse me for the gasoline expense, and I get to know some of the kids who are a part of Ryan's life. Or use some of your time during the school day to pursue an interest of your own. Take a quilting class. Form a book discussion group.

It's a good idea to try to get out of the house some evenings, too. Arnold and I participate in a handbell choir that meets once a week. When the bell choir disbands for the summer, we're going to take dance classes together (I have his firm promise).

Of course, all of these out-of-the-house experiences don't have to be kidless. You can set up regular park and library outings with younger kids, which fully qualify as getting out of the house. Kids love to be outside. I send mine outside as often as possible! Go for family walks or bike rides. Grow an herb or vegetable garden in the backyard. Getting out of the house doesn't always mean going far away.

In fact, it's even possible to have an out-of-house experience right in your own home! You do it by putting aside the chores for a heartbeat or two, while you pursue some totally nonhouse-related activity that interests you. (I said it is possible; I didn't say it is easy.) I know moms who accomplish this by making crafts, writing poetry, or even getting lost in a good book on occasion.

If done properly, staying home can be a great way to get out of the house.

Is anybody out there?

I like a lot of things about our culture. We can pretty much buy anything we want—and if we can't afford to buy something, we can always rent it for a little while. Rent a movie. Rent a roto-tiller. Rent a paddle boat at the park. Why, I even saw an ad in the paper once for a rent-a-wife service!

So, where's the rent-a-friend office? What's their toll-free number?

I think I'm on to something here. I can see infomercials on TV that run in the middle of the day—the kids' naptime (adjusting for different time zones, naturally). We can call it Friend-o-Matic. Lonely moms at home "adopt" other lonely moms. For a small fee, we'll send out pictures, maybe a recipe or two from the adopted mom's kitchen. Then, when the lonely moms call in, we can zap 'em with another offer—for a slight additional fee (at the time of the call only), they can get the works: dark secrets, contents of dresser drawers, whether she puts her toilet paper on the dispenser "over" or "under"— and, of course, her "true" shoe size.

It would work—don't you think?

Well, maybe not.

You understand, of course, that being a lonely mom at home doesn't necessarily mean you're having an identity crisis. But loneliness can be a symptom of that whole lost-lonely-and-going-crazy syndrome (which sends so many moms flying back into the workforce). And since I don't believe Friend-o-Matic infomercials are in our future, we need to think of some other creative ways to overcome this little problem.

Let me introduce you to Beverly, an at-home mom I met some months ago. She had moved to our city two years before—and she still didn't have any friends!

"I hate it here," she told me. "I miss all my friends from where we used to live."

I nodded my head in sympathetic understanding, then gently shared with her the secret I had learned about stay-at-home moms not really staying home. I mean, it makes sense (doesn't it?) that if you are involved in things that are interesting to you, you'll probably meet some pretty interesting people. And since those people are interested in the same things you are. . . Well, you're smart enough to figure out the rest.

RESOURCES FOR STAY-AT-HOME MOMS

MomSense
1311 South Clarkson Street
Denver, CO 80210
(303) 733-5353
   Newsletter for mothers of preschoolers. Write for free quarterly subscription.

Out of the Rat Race
P.O. Box 95341-DMO
Seattle, WA 98145-2341
   Support and tips for moms who left the workplace to come home. Send SASE for free newsletter sample.

The Mommy Times Newsletter
   Quarterly eight-page newsletter for parents of preschoolers to teens. Call 1-800-99-MOMMY for free sample.

Mothering
P.O. Box 1690
Santa Fe, NM 87504
(505) 984-8116
   Strongly family-oriented quarterly magazine with "gentle support" for moms and dads—write or call for subscription information.

Welcome Home
8310A Old Courthouse Road
Vienna, VA 22182
   Magazine for moms at home. Subscription for one year, $18, sample copy, $2.

I didn't see Beverly again, but one day a few months later she phoned me. "I just wanted to let you know," she said, "that I'm much happier here now. I took your advice and joined a couple of groups at my church, and now I have lots of friends!"

I guess I'd have to say here that moms at home are just about as lonely as we choose to be. If you're lonely, you are probably spending a lot of time by yourself, taking care of kids (who—let's face it—are adorable but not very intellectually stimulating), asking the occasional adults you see if they need to go potty. I think it's a safe bet that you'd have a lot better chance of making friends if you went someplace where there were a few other "big" people around.

And people on TV don't count!

WAIT JUST A MINUTE, HERE!

I read an article in a major women's magazine about a mom who "experimented" with coming home. She felt she *should* give it a try—her kids being so little and all. After a few months, she couldn't wait to get back to work. Being at home was driving her crazy!

Too bad for her that I hadn't written this book yet. She could have seen where she was going wrong. One, she totally devoted herself to her kids and quit taking care of herself. Two, she didn't get out of the house. And three, she didn't give staying home enough time.

Now, pay attention here. This is important.

Don't think that just because you were born with ovaries, you automatically know how to do the staying home thing. Or that, because it may be difficult during the first few weeks, you simply weren't "meant" for the stay-at-home life. We don't expect our kids to learn to talk fluently in two or three months after uttering their first "ma-ma," but we expect ourselves to adjust to being at home in a short time. Making a successful transition from a job to being at home full-time can take months, and maybe even years!

It took me an entire year just to *begin* to get an idea of what staying home was all about. I'm now in my third year of being at home and there are still things I'm learning about this new job. It takes time to rebuild your identity! In the business world, this transition period is called the learning curve.

When you get a new paying job, doesn't it take a while to get comfortable with your new duties? I used to train people to use word processing software. I always told the trainees to expect to be uncomfortable with the new program for at least three months—*after* they learned it. It takes that long just to become accustomed to the commands to the point that you don't have to think about which button to push on the computer when you want to do something with it. After the new employee had learned the word processor, it would still take several more months for her to get comfortable with the operations of the company—to know "who's who" and "what's what" and "where's where." And keep in mind that the new employee has plenty of people around to ask questions of. She *might* be really comfortable in the job after about a year.

So, if it takes a year to get comfortable in a paying job, where there are scads of people standing around helping you learn your job and get organized, why would you give yourself any less time to get used to the job of being at home? As a matter of fact, you ought to give yourself *more* time, because there's a good chance you'll be doing it on your own without a huge network of support. Making changes takes effort, and time—and yes, I'll say it—work. You have to give yourself a chance to let go of the past and redefine who you are.

So, take a deep breath. Wait for a while. Be patient with yourself. Give yourself time to work through the learning curve. You might even learn something wonderful about yourself!

I AM SOMEBODY'S MOM

I think we could all agree at this point that if you're willing to *work*, you *can* build a new identity for yourself at home. We could just stop right there and move on to other titillating stay-at-home topics without feeling as if we'd missed anything on the identity agenda.

Still, I cannot let this issue slip by without stating the obvious. Everyone knows that raising kids is the most important job in the world. Did you catch that? It's a *job*. And whether you work outside the home or not, it's your job, because you're the mom.

Even so, raising kids is a temporary job. My mother said something extraordinary to me the day Ryan was born. "It's time to start letting go," she told me.

I was stunned. "Letting go?" I asked. "I've barely even held him yet!"

"Yes, but your job," she said, "is to teach him how to live without you."

I've carried those words around with me for ten years. Those words are a big part of the reason that I came home again, because I realized that right now I have the choice to be with my son. Soon—too soon—I won't have that choice. He'll be off living his own life—ignoring me, forgetting to call and falling in love with *someone else*.

We started off this chapter with that fear we have of just being "somebody's mom." We've talked about how important it is to take care of yourself and your needs, so that you can do a good job of being somebody's mom. The thought occurs to me, however, that one of the best ways I can take care of me is to *not miss* this one and only opportunity I have to be my son's mom. I know myself, and I would miss it if I wasn't at home.

So being here, for me, is worth the trouble of being a little lost and lonely at times, and having to scratch out a new identity or job description for myself. I'm glad, on most days, that I made that choice to be home.

Of course, there are those days when I'm not so sure. You know, the days when everything goes wrong, the kid's trying to expand his boundaries—again—and I feel about as glamorous as the lint trap in the dryer.

Those are the days when I have to sit myself down and give myself a good talking-to.

CHAPTER 10 ✍

GAB SESSION

(What to do when you start talking to yourself.)

First say to yourself what you would be, and then do what you have to do.

EPICTETUS circa A.D. 65–135

JUST LISTEN TO YOURSELF!

It happens. Don't be alarmed. We stay-at-home moms talk to ourselves. Actually, I rather enjoy it! I'm with myself almost constantly. I usually laugh at my jokes, and I hardly ever hurt my feelings. I know exactly what I need to hear. I can be good company for me.

But I can also be my worst enemy. Sometimes—when I least expect it—I say mean things to myself. Unsympathetic things. Things like, "You're fat! You're useless! You can't do anything right!"

At those times, I ought to also say, "Just listen to yourself!" I wonder what I would think if I could really hear what I was saying?

If you're a stay-at-home mom, the next time someone asks you, "Do you work?" *just listen to yourself.*

Do you hear what you're saying?
Just listen to what Emily is saying.

Surprise Party

Emily felt Jack's hand on her elbow as they walked into the hotel ballroom. She bit her lower lip, immediately regretting it. *There goes the lipstick*, she thought, and sighed.

A look around the room made her glad she had worn the black velvet. Everyone was wearing black. *They're all so elegant!* she thought. *Am I the only woman here in a cocktail-length dress?* She started chewing off her lipstick again.

"Jack—there you are!" A tall man with gray hair moved toward them through the crowd, lifting his champagne glass over the head of a svelte woman dressed in a floor-length sequined gown.

"Hello, Ted!" Jack said. As the men shook hands, Emily couldn't take her eyes off that sequined gown and its wearer. The woman's hair was perfect—like something in a magazine. *She's so lucky,* Emily thought, remembering her own struggle with the blow dryer a couple of hours ago. She had been pleased with the result—until now.

"I'd like you to meet my wife," Jack said, pulling her toward him. "Emily, this is Ted."

Emily looked up at the tall man next to her husband. "Hello, Ted," she said. "Jack's told me a lot about you."

"Oh, really? He hasn't said a thing about you!"

Laughter erupted from both men. Emily tried to shoot an oh-you're-so-cute glare in Jack's direction.

"Hey," said Jack, "Why don't the two of you get acquainted and I'll go get us some drinks!"

Before she knew what had happened, Jack was walking off toward the bar, leaving her standing next to a suddenly silent Ted. He smelled like Old Spice, which surprised her. He seemed more the type to use one of those high-priced designer fragrances she saw advertised on TV.

"Well, uh, Emily," Ted began, "what do you do? I mean, do you work?"

"Oh, no," she said. "I'm just a mom. Our three kids keep me pretty busy."

"Yes, yes, I can imagine."

An awkward silence filled the space between them.

"Do you have any children?" Emily asked in a voice that sounded too bright.

"Me? Oh, sure. Four of 'em! Wife didn't stay home with 'em, though. She's always been very career-minded. Can't get that woman to do anything I say!" He laughed again—at some private joke or something, Emily supposed. She looked around to see if Jack was anywhere near. No such luck.

"What kind of work does your wife do?" *Just what I wanted—to hear about some other woman who actually has a life.*

"She owns her own consulting firm. Very successful. That's her—right over there." He pointed across the room to Ms. Perfect-Hair-in-Floor-Length-Sequins.

"She's lovely," Emily said. *Why did I wear this dress?*

"Come on, I'll introduce you!" Ted grabbed Emily's elbow and practically dragged her across the room.

What do I possibly have to say to her? Emily thought. *I wish I was anywhere but here!*

Do you hear what I hear?

Emily has a lot of, shall we say, *interesting* things to say, doesn't she? We all talk to ourselves (even moms who have jobs outside the home). And a lot of what we say to ourselves is negative!

If you don't believe me, maybe you'll believe Shad Helmstetter, Ph.D., author of *What to Say When You Talk to Your Self* and *The Self-Talk Solution*. In the former book, he noted, "Leading behavioral researchers have told us that as much as *seventy-seven percent* of everything we think is negative, counter-productive, and works against us."

But let's focus on some of the negative ways moms at home talk to themselves. Okay. I'll rephrase that. Let's talk about some of the negative ways stay-at-home moms talk to *ourselves*. If I'm going to lecture you, I might as well include myself— because I'm pretty good at this negative self-talk stuff!

You heard Emily doing it. "I'm just a mom." "I don't work." She's worried about having to meet Ted's accomplished career-oriented wife. Emily didn't think it consciously, but underneath it all she feels inferior, less than capable . . . maybe even worthless! All her life she's wanted to be a mom—and now that she's accomplished that goal, she's, well, ashamed. Not of being a mom! No! Emily's ashamed—sometimes—of being a mom *at home*.

Do you ever feel that way? Do you ever allow yourself to think that way? Have you ever heard yourself saying things to yourself that reflect that attitude? I know I have. If you haven't felt that way, well, good for you!

I suppose this might be a good time to forge ahead into an exhaustive study of *why* moms at home are afflicted with such negative self-talk. It must be *somebody's* fault! We could blame it on the men (that's always fun), or the kids (they can just sap *everything* out of a mom!), or even other women (those who say you're nobody if you don't work outside the home).

But let's not. Instead of trying to fix the blame for our negative self-talk on someone or something else, let's try something new, and (dare I say it?) . . . *bold*. We can admit that we do talk negatively to ourselves, and then see if we can't figure out something better to do with our thoughts and our words. Maybe we can even learn to "talk nice" to ourselves!

"I DON'T WORK"

When I was in college, I learned several useful acronyms. LIFO is an accounting term meaning "last in, first out." You know—the same criteria a lot of companies use when "downsizing." NBD—"no big deal." And, of course, you're familiar with RSVP and BYOB. But my favorite little acronym is one I learned in a computer programming class. GIGO (pronounced "guy-go"). "Garbage in, garbage out."

Now what GIGO means in computer programming terms is this: A computer is a machine, nothing more, nothing less. It can only do what people tell it to do. And if you tell a computer to do something it doesn't "understand," you won't get any useful information out of it. Garbage in, garbage out.

Emily's self-talk is a prime example of GIGO activity. "I don't work." Poor Emily. If she had the opportunity to read this book, she would realize that she *does* work. All mothers work!

But let's get back to the garbage. (You might say we're going to dish some real dirt here!) What do you do with your household garbage? I recycle some of mine—things like plastic bottles and newspapers. But a lot of our household garbage eventually makes its way *to the dump*. In other words, we get rid of it. If we didn't get rid of it, we wouldn't like the resulting smell and mess.

I'm sorry to have to be so graphic here, but sometimes it's necessary. Moms at home have been recycling a certain piece of garbage that needs to go to the dump. We recycle it every time one of us says, "I don't work." We tell ourselves that we don't work, then we tell other people that we don't work. Garbage in, garbage out!

Unfortunately, "I don't work" isn't the only self-talk garbage we recycle. We tell ourselves so many negative things: "I'm ugly." "I always forget things!" "I'm so stupid!" Dr. Helmstetter says, "You will become what you think about most." Think about *that* for a minute. It's scary.

On the other hand, becoming what you think about most can also be very exciting—depending on what you're thinking about. I say let's haul all that negative stuff to the dump and get rid of it. Let's stop recycling statements that ought to be thrown away. Then we can try a different, *positive* approach to the way we talk to and about ourselves! We can call it PIPO—positive in, positive out.'' What have we got to lose (besides a lot of garbage)?

PIPO Practice (Positive In, Positive Out)

Practice the following statements, so that the next time someone asks you, "Do you work?" you'll be prepared with a positive answer!

- "Why, yes, I do. I work at home."
- "Yes, I work. I'm raising my children."
- "Yes, I'm a crisis management specialist. What do *you* do?"
- "Yes, I work very hard. Do you work?"
- "I'm a mother! All mothers work!"

Consider starting off your day with some statements like these:

- "Today is a great day!"
- "I *love* being at home!"
- "I'm a very positive person!"
- "Oh, look—it's raining! Goody!"
- "Laundry is my best friend." (Hey—it's worth a shot!)

"She's So Lucky!"

Envy. It's one of those yucky little four-letter words. Envy is what we often experience when we compare our lives to someone else's.

Saying, ''She's so lucky'' to yourself isn't so bad on its own.

But usually when I say something like that, what I really mean is, "She's so lucky—*and I'm not!*"

I'm particularly fond of comparing myself to my sister, who's really lucky. She's blond—and I'm not. She's one of the clean house people—and I'm not. She's taller than I am, thinner than I am—and she was way more popular than I was in school. Her house is bigger. Her car is nicer. She travels more. Sometimes I look at her and think, "Boy, does she have the perfect life— and I don't!"

Then, one day, a miracle occurred. My sister said to me, "I've always been so jealous of you!"

What? Miss A-Place-for-Everything" was jealous of Miss Just-Throw-It-Under-The-Bed? It had never occurred to me that anyone else—especially my "lucky" sister—might compare herself to me, and come up short. I honestly don't remember what she was jealous of (and neither, conveniently, does she). But I was so astonished that she was jealous at all, it got me to thinking.

I realized that I had wasted a lot of time worrying about the fact that I am not like my sister. I was so busy beating myself up because she has some qualities I can only wish for, that I forgot I have some pretty nice qualities of my own—qualities she (or someone else) might even envy. Besides, I failed to recognize one very important thing: I'm not *supposed* to be like my sister—or anyone else for that matter! She and I are simply different, like apples and oranges. And *everyone* knows you can't compare apples and oranges.

So, if you're comparing yourself or your life to someone else's, stop wasting energy on that effort right now. Maybe you're a terrific banana! The point is, there's no one else on this earth exactly like you. Sure. Maybe that mom over there has a big house and seemingly perfect kids. Her life *looks* good. But looks can be deceiving.

You see, the other problem with comparing ourselves to other people is that we're not even comparing ourselves to the reality of what that other person is. Take an attractive used car on the dealer's lot, for example. From a distance it looks really great—

bright, shiny, and all that good stuff. Perfect. Then you get a little closer. There's a scratch on the door. The inside smells a little funny. There's a cigarette burn in the upholstery, and one of the floor mats is missing. Maybe the car still looks good up close, but when you try to drive it you find out it's a clunker. Bad engine. No spark plugs. Sometimes something can look really good on the outside and be all messed up on the inside.

It's the same with people. We see someone across a crowded room and she looks perfect, like when Emily sees Ted's wife with her great hair and floor-length sequins. She feels inferior to this woman because her life looks so good—from a distance. But if Emily takes the time to get to know Ted's wife, she might discover that her life isn't as perfect as it appears to be from a distance. How can Emily tell, by looking across the room, that Ted's wife found a lump in her breast yesterday morning, or that she and Ted are on the verge of divorce? She can't. And neither can we.

I feel obliged to point out, here, that moms with jobs face the same hazard when comparing themselves to moms at home. It may seem to a working mom that her friend who stays home has the perfect life. She might even envy her friend's apparently carefree existence. I hope moms with jobs are beginning to realize that, in many ways, being at home isn't any easier than having a job.

It's dangerous to compare ourselves to others. We need to recognize that everyone has problems to deal with—their problems are just different from ours. Part of the whole issue of making choices about your life is: Which problems are you going to choose? Nothing and no one is perfect! My life at home works better for me and my family than working outside the home did, but I still have problems. What's more important is that I'm living the life I've chosen—complete with its joys and its burdens. Some moms choose the burdens of working outside the home, because that's what works for them.

At least now, when I look at those moms, I think to myself, "She works hard at her job—and so do I."

"I'M JUST A MOM"

Emily said, "I'm just a mom." Oh, really. Just a mom.

The person in the Oval Office doesn't say, "I'm just the president of the United States."

The guy living in the Vatican doesn't mumble, "Oh, yeah, I'm just the pope."

Nothing we accomplish in this life is more important than what we accomplish as mothers. We have been entrusted with an awesome obligation—to raise our kids so that someday (we hope) they won't need us to take care of them anymore. (If we're lucky, they'll take care of us!) If enough of us do our job right, the world will be a better place when our kids are out there in it.

The other night, Ryan and I were out for an evening stroll. He's in the fourth grade now, and in California that means he's building a model of one of the Spanish missions for a class project. As we walked together in the cool evening air, Ryan bounced his mission-building ideas off me.

"I could make a little brick mold," he said, "and make a bunch of little bricks and build the walls that way!"

"Yes, you could do that. It might take a long time."

Ryan walked quietly for a moment. "Maybe I could make the walls out of Styrofoam," he offered as an alternative.

We continued to walk and talk this way, when, suddenly, he reached over and put his arm around my waist and laid his head against my arm.

"I love my mom," he said.

Returning the one-armed hug, I said, "I love my son, too." It was one of those rare moments in time—the kind you try to hold in your heart and cherish always.

Just a mom, indeed!

IF YOU CAN'T SAY SOMETHING NICE . . .

Okay. We've talked about getting rid of some of the garbage we recycle in our words. We've practiced PIPO—"positive in, positive out.'' We've even discovered that we are each unique and special and incomparable.

So—you're all set. Right? The next time someone asks you what you do for a living, you'll be ready for them!

Or maybe, just maybe, you'll still be feeling a little uncomfortable about what to say. Maybe you won't have had enough time to practice PIPO and you'll be tempted to say something negative. Should this happens to you, let me offer you a last-ditch strategy.

If you can't say something nice (about yourself), don't say anything at all! Just smile and ask that person something about him or her. Comment on the great food or the lovely music. No one ever said that just because someone asks you a question, you have to answer it. Okay—if you're on the witness stand in a court of law, you have to. But it's highly unusual for anyone to make you swear to ''tell the whole truth and nothing but the truth'' as you enter a party or other social gathering. Go ahead and be a little mysterious.

Now, I am not advocating dishonesty or saying that you should purposely mislead someone about what you do. I'm just saying that if you have a hard time being positive about your role as a mom at home, at least let the negative comments rest for a while. It's what we tell our kids—''If you can't say something nice, don't say anything at all.'' It's good advice. We should listen to ourselves!

Anyway, remaining silent when someone asks you a question can be a very beneficial skill to possess, especially when the question begins something like, ''Would you like to volunteer to . . .''

CHAPTER 11

"READ MY LIPS"

(Say this with me, slowly . . .
"O-ver-com-mit-ment.")

Just say No.

—Nancy Reagan

Health alert!

The notion that moms at home have gobs and oodles of free time has permeated our culture. This unfortunate misconception has given rise to a terrible malady—a highly contagious and infectious virus extremely prevalent among mothers who choose to stay at home. The virus is so contagious that it can be, and usually is, transmitted over telephone wires. Symptoms are manifest in the speech patterns of the infected. They begin to say things like, "Sure, I'll do that," and "Okay, I guess," and "Well, since nobody else can . . ." These initial signals are generally followed by a secondary, more telltale indication of the disease: The infected person hangs up the phone and begins to mumble to herself, "Why did I say yes?"

The dreaded disease? Why-did-I-say-yes-itis. Its source: the volunteerism virus.

Be on the lookout for this virus! Otherwise, you might end up like Karen here. She thinks she has time for . . .

Just One More Thing

"Hello?" Karen answered the phone just as she placed the last bag of groceries on the counter.

"Hi, Karen! This is Julie. Do you have a minute?"

Karen looked around at her kitchen counters, covered with groceries that needed to be put away.

"Sure, I have a minute. How are you?"

"Oh, I'm just fine. Listen, I need to ask you for a favor."

"A favor?" Karen sloughed her purse off her shoulder and hung it over the corner of a kitchen chair. "What do you need?"

"Oh, not much, really," Julie answered. "We're gearing up for a fund drive at the school and I was wondering if you'd be in charge of a monthly bake sale. All you have to do is call people a few days before the bake sale and remind them to bring something on that day."

Sounds harmless enough, Karen thought. *I guess I have time for this.* "I'd be happy to. What's the first date?"

"A week from tomorrow. Oh—and could you pick up the cashbox from my house that morning? I'd feel better if you were handling all the cash."

"You want me to run the bake sale, too?"

"Well, it's kind of hard to be in charge if you're not there!" Julie said with a little laugh.

"Well—okay. Karen noticed a pain between her shoulder blades. "What time should I pick up the cashbox?"

"We leave pretty early in the mornings. Can you be here at 6:30?"

Karen took a deep breath. "That's a little early for me,

but"—she rubbed her forehead (which was starting to hurt)—"I guess I can do that."

"Great! All the paperwork you need will be inside the box. Just add up all the money and fill out the cash forms—and, you know, just separate out all the bills and coins and stuff."

"Paperwork?" Karen definitely had a headache. And her shoulders hurt. The air around her began to feel unusually warm. *I forgot to buy more aspirin at the store*, she thought, looking at all the sacks of groceries.

"Oh—and just one more thing," said Julie. "I have to make the deposit the first thing the next day, so if you could run that cashbox back by my house I would really appreciate it. I'll be home at about 9:30 that night. Okay?"

"Sure, why not?" Karen answered. Anything to get this woman off the phone. "Look, Julie, I gotta go now. I think I might have a cold coming on or something."

"Oh, well, you'd better get some rest! See you next week!"

Karen hung up the phone. She sat down in the chair. She looked at all those groceries, and suddenly felt as if she had no energy to deal with them.

I'm definitely coming down with something, she thought.

THE VIRUS SPREADS

When I first became an at-home mom, I believed the free time myth. Remember those coming-home fantasies? By the time I saw the light and was freed from my misinterpretation of reality, I had volunteered for and resigned from several activities and organizations.

Like Karen, I had caught why-did-I-say-yes-itis. My motives were pure, because I truly wanted to "do good" and help out everyone who asked me. But the results were often less than perfect.

First, I volunteered to help my son's second grade during their reading time. The kids would bring assignments to me and I would make sure they had answered the questions correctly. Then I'd give them a gold star and they'd go off to read another story. The time commitment was minimal, only two or three times per week, maybe an hour in the classroom. Of course, I'm not including commute time. And, well, that doesn't include "getting dressed to be seen in public" time. Still, I really enjoyed being in the classroom. I thought, this volunteering stuff is a snap.

The next responsibility I took on made me more susceptible to the virus. I agreed to be in charge of an annual community concert series based at my church. All I had to do, it seemed, was to arrange all the concerts, design the concert brochure, go to umpteen meetings, be at the facility early on the day of the concert to let everyone in, stay during the concert to make certain air conditioning or heating was properly set, and stay late after the concert and put everything back in place and lock up the building. Piece of cake.

It was when the next volunteering opportunity came along that I actually caught the virus. I received a phone call (first warning sign—although I didn't know it then) from the chairperson of the church's women's board asking me to be board secretary. All I had to do was go to the once-a-month meeting, take minutes, and type them up afterward for the chairperson.

Then I joined the committee to plan the annual church women's retreat. Seemed like a natural extension of my other duties. The meetings were once or twice a month.

I've always been involved in music, so I joined a small band as one of their singers. That group met once a week.

School newsletter? No problem! Building committee? A snap! Sell school lunch tickets? You got it!

It was also during this time that I began to meet on a weekly basis with a group of local writers to read and critique our writing projects. I was invincible. There was nothing I couldn't do! I had free time!

Boy, was I wrong. Within months my volunteer commitments started dropping like flies.

FREE TIME VS. FLEX TIME

Stay-at-home moms have all the free time in the world, right?

Wrong. Stay-at-home moms have *flex* time. It's important that we get that down right now, because there's a big difference between *free* time and *flex* time.

Having free time means there is nothing else on your schedule (at least nothing *important*); you are "free" to do whatever you want—or to do nothing at all!

Having flex time means you have some flexibility in choosing when to do the many important things you must do every day.

Stay-at-home moms have very little, if any, free time. I've proven this scientifically. I made a schedule of my daily activities to see just how much free time I have. I thought maybe I'd come up with, say, ten minutes a day of free time. My plan was to make this big point about not getting too excited about having a lot of free time when you decide to stay home.

What I discovered, however, is that in my daily schedule I never get to the "free time" part. I'm always busy doing things for other people, or taking care of the house, or fulfilling some obligation or another. Of course, if I'm totally honest (and that *is* the goal here), I should have listed taking care of the house last, because you already know it's not my favorite thing—and when I don't have time for everything, that's the item I bump off my list. And if I'm really going to come clean (pardon the pun), I have to tell you that I might goof off occasionally, but I can't really count that as free time because I *ought* to be doing something else. There's always more than enough stuff that needs to be done, that isn't getting done, that's waiting for me to get it done.

But I do have flex time. Although many of the things on my "must do" list are inflexible (like when I leave in the morning to take Ryan to school), I have blocks of time during my day where I may choose which obligation to fulfill at that moment. Take today, for example. Because it happens to be a school holiday, I had the luxury of sleeping in an extra thirty minutes this morning. Okay, maybe it was an hour. Don't distract me.

Anyway, when I woke up this morning I got my morning caffeine and headed straight for the computer. I usually don't get to sit down and work on my writing until midmorning. It's nice to have the flexibility to fit my work into my schedule when it's convenient and comfortable, and I really enjoy that the schedule doesn't have to be the same every day.

But please, just let go of this idea of having "free" time. It simply doesn't exist! We all have the same twenty-four hours each day—stay-at-home moms don't get any extra hours. I know, it seems like stay-at-homers have more time, because we haven't obligated ourselves to the fixed schedule of an employer. But that doesn't mean we don't have obligations, or that our time is less valuable than someone's who works outside the home.

Also, do not confuse being flexible with being idle. That old saying, "A man works from sun to sun, but a woman's work is never done," didn't come from your granny's imagination. Stay-at-home moms are always "on-duty," because we never leave our workplace. We live, eat, sleep, and play in it, and there's always something that needs to be done.

Anyone who's been at home with the kids for any length of time has experienced this feeling. Even David, a stay-at-home *dad* in Chicago, agrees:

> *I often feel overwhelmed by all the stuff I have to do around the house. Trying to juggle all the different hats I have to wear is hard work and, many times, frustrating. I hate it when being with and caring for my kids takes a backseat to "chores." But reality dictates sometimes I have to get things done during the day with the kids in tow. [Sometimes] I just stop where I am, and tell myself, 'There will always be grass to cut. There will always be laundry to do.*

There will always be bills to pay or filing to be done. Getting them done at this exact moment won't make any difference in the long run. But my kids will only have today to share with me right now.

NO GUTS, NO GLORY

It finally sunk in. I didn't have free time. My time was *not* available to whoever wanted it merely for the asking. I had to start making some serious choices about how to best spend my at-home time.

But how to choose? How was I supposed to figure out where to donate my very valuable time? How could I protect myself from the volunteerism virus?

I came up with a three-step plan to evaluate adding a new activity to my schedule. Whenever someone calls and asks me to volunteer for some worthy "only I could possibly do it and if I don't I'll be letting everyone down" activity, I start with . . .

STEP ONE
"Let me think about it and I'll get back to you."

It's very important, in the early stages, to buy time.

Next, because I believe in keeping things sequential, I execute step two: I think about it.

STEP TWO
Think about it.

You may think step two is a no-brainer, but for someone who truly thinks she can do everything, and who wants to keep everyone else happy all the time, the "thinking about it" stage is very important! As I think about what I've been asked to do, I try to pay attention to how I feel about doing that particular thing. I try to imagine myself involved in the activity, going to the meetings, spending more time away from the family.

I think about all the things I have already committed myself to do. It's easy to get sucked into a new volunteer activity because you're told that it only takes X hours a week or Y hours a month. You think to yourself, "I have that many hours I could devote to this very worthy cause!" But if you add X hours for this activity to the Z hours you've already promised somewhere else, the picture looks a little different. That's because it's the *big* picture.

After giving the matter a sufficient amount of thought, I am ready for step three. I ask myself, what is my gut feeling about doing this particular thing?

STEP THREE
What is my gut feeling?

Step three separates the moms from the wimps. It's possible to get all the way through step two and still waver on a decision because you feel you *should* do this thing. And maybe you should. But if your gut tells you, in step three, that you don't *want* to do it, saying yes will only make you miserable, you probably won't do a good job, and you might even end up bowing out later because it's so hard to find the time to do things you don't want to do.

This three-step process simplified my life. It helped me to clarify which things were important to me and which were not. I discovered that some of my volunteer activities were more important to me than others, and some I didn't care for at all. For example, I kept the school activities. Hanging around your child's school is a great way to be "in the know" about what's *really* going on there. Besides, it's fun to get to know the teachers and staff. And I do enjoy the kids! Also, since one of the reasons I came home in the first place was to spend more time with my son, investing some of my flex time at his school was a great way to invest myself in him.

Remember, too, that saying no to a request to volunteer isn't going to be the end of the world for anybody. In fact, I believe I'm doing people a favor when I say no to things I don't really want (in my gut) to do. They don't need a second-rate volunteer whose heart isn't in the project! My saying no clears the way for that person who just can't wait to get his or her teeth into that activity. By bowing out gracefully, I am leaving the door open for the absolute perfect person to do that job.

Now, *that* takes guts.

Vocab rehab

Another good way to protect yourself from catching why-did-I-say-yes-itis is to clean out your phrase and vocabulary storage areas. Many phrases that we pick up during our lifetimes carry with them a dormant strain of the volunteerism virus, which can be activated by the introduction of solicitous telephone calls into their delicate environment. By removing such phrases from your vocabulary storage areas, you can greatly reduce the chance of infection. The phrases to watch out for fall into three distinct categories: "I should," "I'm the only one" and the ever-insidious "I don't know what to say."

"I should . . ."

This phrase and variations of it is Why-did-I-say-yes-itis waiting to happen. Look also, when searching for this category, for "I ought to" and "I feel obligated."

There are a great many things in this life that we *must* do. We must eat. We must sleep. We must dispose of dirty diapers. But generally, when we begin to say things like "I should," we are talking about something that *someone else* thinks would be a good use of our time.

Think about it. Do you *ever* say "I should" about something you really want to do? I can't imagine myself saying, "I should go to the mall and try on some new clothes." No way! I say, "Hey, I think I'll go check out the new shipments at my favorite store!"

Saying "I should" when discussing a volunteer activity is a flashing neon signal that you *shouldn't* do it. Really.

"I'm the only one . . ."

"I'm the only one who can do this," and its sibling phrases, "There's nobody else!" and "If I don't do it, it won't get done," are simply loaded with the volunteerism virus. These phrases are usually followed by an "I should" statement, further exposing you to the virus and the subsequent dreaded disease.

These phrases are born of an overinflated sense of self-importance, and would be worth getting rid of for that reason alone. Such phrases infect us with the volunteerism virus, resulting in our doing something we really don't want to do. They also cause us to stand in the way of someone who does want to do it and would most assuredly do a better job.

Please allow me to illustrate. Recently, I was asked to be in charge of the music at our annual church women's retreat for the third year in a row. I wanted to do it. Everyone even said I was good at leading the music on these retreats. And I felt that I was the only one who could do it.

I had to say no, however, because I couldn't fit even one more thing into my schedule. I worried. I fretted. What would they do without me? After all, I was the only one who could do it . . . right? Almost immediately another volunteer stepped forward to take my place. Judi not only did a terrific job with the music, but she also wrote a song specifically for the retreat—something that I had never even thought of doing.

So relax. There are other people in the world who not only can do what you can do, they can do it better!

"I don't know what to say . . ."

At first glance, you might not think this phrase would carry the volunteerism virus, and it is precisely for this reason that it is so very dangerous. When a person calls you on the phone

PRACTICE SAYING NO

If you have a hard time turning down anyone or anything, practice the following in your spare time. Try writing these phrases down on sticky notes and stick them on your bathroom mirror. Or make a tape so you can hear your own voice saying:

1. No.
2. I'm honored to be considered, but I can't.
3. No.
4. No, but thank you for asking.
5. No.
6. I wish I could, but it's impossible.
7. No.
8. Thank you for thinking of me, but I can't.
9. No.

and tries to transmit the virus to you, the longer you stay on the line the more open you are to infection. This phrase lengthens time of exposure.

You are far better off to simply say No as quickly as possible, and get off the phone before the virus has a chance to spread!

YOUR TIME VALUE

Although I do believe that Why-did-I-say-yes-itis is a dangerous and vile disease, please don't think that I'm against volunteerism altogether. The trick is to create and maintain the delicate balance between volunteer activities and other responsibilities. Part of the privilege of being home is having the opportunity to help others with your time and energy. It won't help anyone, however, if you find yourself overcommitted and overworked, trying to fulfill obligations better served by someone else.

There is a great deal of joy and fulfillment in giving yourself to volunteer activities which you have a heart for. Everybody wins.

To be able to choose wisely, you must know things such as where your heart is, and how much time you can devote to activities outside the home. And figuring that out is going to take some work. But that's okay. All mothers work.

CHAPTER 12 ∞

THE NO-FUSS BUDGET

(Financial finagling for the fiscally frugal)

Even though work stops, expenses run on.
CATO THE ELDER, circa 234–149 B.C.

WHO CAN AFFORD TO STAY HOME?

Money. We keep coming back to it, don't we? That's because money permeates the very fiber of our existence. I don't know one mother who doesn't want more of it. Well, there's Mother Teresa, but I don't know her. Most of the moms I know are struggling just to get the bills paid.

The very best financial strategy that I know of that may enable you to stay home is to try, just as hard as you can, to be independently wealthy. If you're not currently independently wealthy, but want to use this strategy so you, too, can be an at-home mom, try one of the following:

Financial Strategy—Independent Wealth

1. Inherit—it is extremely helpful to already have, or to acquire, some rich relatives. Countless women have, both cur-

rently and in the past, married into and/or for money. I'm not making a value judgment here, just stating a well-known and well-documented fact.

2. Win the lottery or sweepstakes. (Hey, a one-in-twenty-billion chance is still a chance.)
3. Make friends with a good-hearted philanthropist. Good friends. *Very* good friends.
4. Invent something similar to the Topsy Tail, which you can manufacture for pennies and sell for $20 a pop. Then sell millions of them.

Independent wealth is a handy strategy for some moms, but, unfortunately, it is not an option open to most of us. But never fear—more financial help is on the way. Let me tell you about Sue. Just watch how she works out some of her money struggles. (Please note, the name in this story has been changed to protect the author from undue embarrassment.)

Bills, Bills, Bills (and I Don't Mean Williams)

Sue sat down at the kitchen table and took a deep breath. She looked at the pile of bills in front of her. A knot began to form in her stomach.

"I need a soda," she said aloud, even though no one else was in the house to hear her. "Can't pay bills without my caffeine, now, can I?" She walked across the kitchen and pulled a clean glass out of the dishwasher, then went over to the freezer for some ice.

We're probably the only family on this street without an ice maker, she thought as she opened the freezer. The cold air rushed out while Sue stood there looking at the empty ice bin. She made a mental note to talk to Jim about having an ice maker installed.

Four ice trays and five minutes later, she was back at the table with her soda.

"Okay. Bills, pen, calculator, checkbook. I'm ready."

She looked again at the pile of bills in front of her. *But I'm not ready,* she thought. *I hate paying bills. I hate wondering if there will be enough money. Why did I ever promise Jim I would do this?*

She thought back to a conversation they had six months ago. "If you quit your job," Jim said, "would you be willing to take over writing out the checks for the bills? That would really free up some of my time at home."

"Sure, I can do that!" she answered. After all, she could write checks, couldn't she? Anyway, it was worth it to be there for her kids when they came home from school.

But it hadn't been as easy as she thought. There never seemed to be enough money to cover everything, and Sue was starting to wonder if coming home had been such a good idea.

I've got to figure out how to save more money! she thought, reaching for the first bill. It was from MasterCard. "Let's see. Balance due, $2,320.50," she read. *Gee, the balance was never this high when I was working,* she thought. "Minimum payment due, $45. Hey, we can handle that!" She reviewed the charges from the previous month. There were several items from their weekend trip to the lake—hotel, boat and ski rental, meals—which totaled up to about $600. A little smile crept onto Sue's face as she thought about the fun the family had out on the water. Those kids were fish! The fond memory comforted her as she wrote out a check to Mastercard for $45.

"Okay, what's next?" she said as she picked up a bill with a Visa heading across the top. "Balance due, $1,832.46. Minimum payment, $25." She picked up her pen. *This might not be so bad after all,* she thought.

The federal solution

I—uh, I mean, *Sue*—is in dangerous territory. She is on the verge of embracing a financial strategy that I call the federal solution. Sue doesn't recognize the danger, however, because so many of her friends are doing the same thing. (She thinks there is safety in numbers, but, there's *no* safety in *these* numbers!) This strategy is extremely popular, and I think you'll see why as you follow along with these simple steps:

Financial Strategy—the Federal Solution

1. Plan a budget that you can't possibly afford in your wildest dreams.
2. Revise the numbers down somewhat.
3. Announce proudly and publicly that you've cut your budget by 10 percent.
4. Live off bank loans and credit cards, and avoid bothersome discussions on subjects such as "balance."

The federal solution is a great way to finance any level of lifestyle to which you would like to become accustomed. Trust me. I know. Money is no object because you simply increase your debt load when you want something new. It's great—up to a point. You might have noticed how nervous Sue was about paying the bills. Maybe, deep down inside, she knows there must be a better way.

Cash on the barrel head

That better way is the final strategy we will discuss here. I should warn you—it's not as prevalent as the federal solution and not as convenient as independent wealth. Many would even call it an "old-fashioned" idea. What we're talking about here—now, brace yourself—is *living within your means*. Sounds radical, I know, but take heart. The execution of this strategy is very simple:

Financial Strategy—Live Within Your Means

1. Spend less money than the family brings in.

Wow. What a concept.

The question, for most stay-at-home moms, is: Is living within your means really possible? I mean, does anyone actually do that sort of thing—these days?

Making Do

Okay. *She* did it. But how can *we* do it? How do we make the money last longer than the month? How do families survive on one paycheck?

Well, we start by making do.

Gwen Weising is a mom who did, and she wrote about it in her book, *Finding Dollars for Family Fun.* She talks about making the decision, when her children were small, to stay home with them even though the family was very poor. "It was tough," she shares. "Life would have been easier, from a monetary standpoint, if I had taken a job. But we made it through that time."

Amy Dacyczn is another mom who learned to live within her means. She publishes a monthly, 8-page newsletter called *The Tightwad Gazette.* You can receive a subscription by sending your name, address, and $12 to: The Tightwad Gazette, RR1 Box 3570, Leeds, ME 04263.

My parents always made do. As a matter of fact, they're still making do. What's that old saying? Use it up, wear it out, make it do, or do without! I'll go out on a limb here and say that this kind of attitude isn't wildly popular in today's society. But people who lived through the Depression and the war years learned to make do, because they didn't have any other choices. My mom told me how, when she was a girl, she and the other girls in town would walk along the road and pick up discarded cigarette packages. Then they would peel the foil from the paper and make a ball of foil—because every single scrap of metal available was needed for the war effort. Now, *that's* making do! (I should probably mention that I believe this story, unlike the one my dad—and yours?—tells about walking barefoot through the snow five miles to school.)

Face it. We're spoiled. We're accustomed to solving our problems, at times, by running to the nearest retail outlet. Depressed? Go shopping! Is something broken? Go buy a new one! No cash? Use that plastic power!

Do you realize that before credit cards, people actually *waited* to buy the things they wanted and needed? They *had* to—unless they could convince someone to give them a loan—and who wants to make a trip to the bank just because they're in the mood for a nice dinner out? Just yesterday my husband told me we need to take our cars in for service. Since I balance the checkbook, he wanted to know if there was enough money in the account, or if he should use the credit card. Fortunately (today) there's enough money in the account. But I realized how easily we turn to plastic when the cash gets short. It's as natural as breathing in, and breathing out. And that's scary!

PUT THOSE CREDIT CARDS ON ICE

If you find it difficult to restrain yourself from whipping out your credit card for any reason whatsoever, try this little tip I learned from a wise bank executive years ago. She told me the bank often shared this advice with its customers suffering from the credit card crunch:

Put your credit cards in a plastic container, then fill the container with water. Place the container in the freezer. Your credit cards are still there if you need them for an emergency or for a planned event, but even in the microwave it takes a while to thaw out all that ice.

This little strategy just might cool down some of those spending urges!

After hearing my mom's story, I wondered how we could come so far from a world where children collected aluminum from discarded cigarette packages to the world we know today. But then I realized, with some relief, that some vestige of our parents' money attitudes made it through the haze of our "I want it and I want it now" society. If we can only capture the essence of this legacy, we can make do very nicely, thank you.

GOOD ADVICE

What I'm talking about here is something that you already have available to you. It's so simple you'll wonder why you didn't think of it!

If we want to learn how to live within our means, all we need to do is apply to ourselves the money advice we give to our children:

- You can't have everything you want.
- Money doesn't grow on trees.
- You don't have to buy everything you see.
- You don't have to have something just because your friend has it.
- Everything doesn't always have to be brand new.
- Do you have enough money to buy that?
- We can't afford it!
- You want something? Save up for it!

There. Now that wasn't too hard, was it?

THE BEST THINGS IN LIFE

The fact of the matter is, we do not have to spend money every time we turn around to have a satisfying lifestyle. Not only that, if we are buying everything we think we need, we could be depriving ourselves of some very special "adventures."

When Arnold was out of work this past year, money was tight. We were very careful not to spend any money we didn't absolutely have to. I remember thinking, *Why hadn't we been treating our money this way all along?* But there really wasn't time to bemoan the past because we had other things to worry about: the mortgage, the car payments, utilities, and such. Those little, annoying things. Oh, and eating.

I've already confessed that we have a habit of eating out more than we should—a little tidbit left over from my "working" days. But during this time of financial difficulty, eating out was definitely *out*! I started scrounging in the freezer, and it was amazing. Suddenly we were having home-cooked family meals every night—meals that I was extremely proud of creating from the nooks and crannies of the cupboard. I had a great sense of accomplishment, and we did just fine during that time. Finding something for supper became a great game to me. Some nights we had cereal and toast, and other nights I'd bone a chicken breast and cook it in some rice. The point is, we ate.

But the greater benefit we received from that time was the fact that, every evening, we sat down in our own kitchen and ate together—as a family. Instead of arguing about which fast-food place would get our money, we were sharing our days' activities with one another. It was a wonderful time.

I realize that many of you are quite accomplished at the gentle art of making do. If you are, share your knowledge with others. Share the hidden joys that surprise your life. Maybe if more of us knew about the special things that could happen if we didn't solve every life issue with the checkbook, or the credit card, more of us would have the courage to embark upon the making do adventure.

CHEAP IS *NOT* A FOUR-LETTER WORD!

To begin practicing the fine art of making do, incorporate the following words and phrases into your vocabulary: garage

THE BEST THINGS IN LIFE *ARE* FREE!

- Spring showers.
- Autumn colors.
- Snow "angels."
- Smiles.
- Hugs.
- Kisses.
- Friends.
- Family time.
- The words "I love you."

sales, wholesale clubs, resale stores, thrift shops, homemade, used cars, buying in bulk, freezers, no credit cards, no ATM cards, gardens, generic brands, baby-sitting co-ops.

This is it. The nitty-gritty. The fun stuff.

If you are willing to foster an adventurous spirit, you can save money and still have a happy, healthy lifestyle. The tips offered here are intended to whet your adventurous appetite, to make you want more. It's so much fun to find creative ways to save money! You can do it, too!

One mom shared with me how she uses her coupon savings at the grocery store to finance Christmas. When she writes the check to the store, she makes it out for the total before the coupon savings were deducted. She then takes the coupon savings amount as change in cash, and that money goes into a special Christmas jar at home.

I spend about $100 a week on groceries. That's $5,200 a year. I know I can average 20 percent savings by using coupons, and that's $1,040 saved over the course of the year! $1,040 will buy a lot of little metal cars (and maybe even a nice gift for my husband.) What a wonderful way to collect extra money for the holidays!

Another mom shares that she stretches the budget by diluting frozen concentrated juice more than the can says. She and her husband still enjoy orange juice when it's prepared at a ratio of four to one (four cans of water to one can of concentrate), and the kids like grape and apple juice prepared at a ratio of five to one. It's probably even better for us, since most of us don't drink enough water.

Speaking of water, drink it! It's good for you, it makes you feel good, and it's practically free. When you're thirsty, reach for a glass of water instead of a soda can. You'll be able to see and feel a difference, both in your pocket and in your physical well-being.

Going on a family nature hike? (Another great money-saving family-togetherness adventure!) Instead of buying an expensive can of bug spray, rub the inside of an orange peel on your skin. It works as a great mosquito repellent and it smells good. And you can eat the orange, to boot!

Another great mosquito remedy is vitamin B12. For some reason, mosquitoes don't like B12-flavored blood. So take your vitamins and keep the bugs away, too! I love it.

Borrow! Instead of buying cribs, high chairs, and strollers, check first to see if any friends or family members are willing to let you borrow theirs for the short time you'll be needing those items. When you've having extra guests over, ask them to bring their card tables and folding chairs. Many people are willing to share unused items that are taking up space in their attics or garages.

Raise your insurance deductibles on your car insurance. And don't carry comprehensive and collision coverage on a car that's older than five years and is paid off. Insure your car and home with the same company—you'll get a discount. Buy used cars—let someone else take that first-year depreciation! Banks still give decent loans on used cars, and you can save a lot of money in the long run.

There are literally thousands of ways to save money, and have fun, too! The library shelves are full of books to help you out here. Make your own mayonnaise. Use rice vinegar as a healthy, tasty salad dressing. Make your own croutons. The possibilities are endless, and limited only by your own imagination and creativity!

Making do is really making money. Every dollar you save is a dollar you don't have to earn at a job outside the home.

CHAPTER 13 ∽

CARE PACKAGING

(Every mother needs a survival kit.)

*What we anticipate seldom occurs; what we
least expected generally happens.*
— BENJAMIN DISRAELI, 1837

A MYSTERIOUS ARRIVAL

Ding-dong! You hear your doorbell ring. Opening the front
door, you find a package. It has your name on it. And a
pretty bow.

Oh, goody, you think. *A present. For me!* You wonder what
the occasion is. You look up and down the street in front of
your house, but don't see anyone who could have left this gift.

Picking up the package, you bring it into your front room.
You notice the attractive paper, and the pleasant fragrance ema-
nating from the package—just like your favorite perfume. With
growing excitement and anticipation you open the envelope that
has your name written on it. Inside the envelope you find a tiny
key—no card—no clue to where this mysterious package came
from. You tuck the key back into the envelope.

As you carefully remove the pretty bow, the wrapping falls

away to reveal a beautiful polished wooden box with a hinged lid. You try to lift the lid, but it doesn't budge. Of course—the key! Admiring your astute assessment of the situation, you pull the key out of the envelope again. The tiny key fits into a keyhole just below the box lid. The keyhole's intricate brass plate is the only decoration on the box.

As you turn the key, you hear a soft *click*. *Oh, boy! This is fun! I wonder what's inside?* The lid opens easily. Inside the box you see pastel-colored shredded packing tissue. On the top, nestled gently amid the tissue, is a card that reads: "Care Package." Moving the card aside, you find beneath it . . .

A Map

Unfolding the paper map, you see that it is a floor plan of your home, with lines and arrows drawn in many of the hallways and through the doors. *Not exactly what I expected,* you think. *It reminds me of one of those fire escape maps.* You notice some writing in the lower left corner of the map:

> *This map will help you to remember how to get out of your house. Post near the TV. It's also useful in case of fire (but don't wait for a fire to use it!).*

Refolding the map, you place it on the floor next to the box. Another item catches your attention. You reach into the box and pull out . . .

A Tape Recorder

It's one of those small, personal dictation recorders, you think. On the front of it is taped a note, which you, naturally, read:

> *Carry this recorder in your pocket. It will turn on automatically and record the things you are saying.*

Purpose: to help you remember to speak positively and with respect to yourself and to others.

You shudder a little when you think about what else the recorder might capture on tape. But then you say to yourself, *This will be a good reminder to watch what I say.* You tuck the recorder into your pocket and peer into the box again. Digging through the tissue, you pull out . . .

A Calendar

You pick up the calendar. It's one of those pocket-size ones that would fit in your purse. On the front of the calendar you see these words:

Refer to this calendar whenever someone asks you to volunteer for something. Say yes only to things that you are able to add to the calendar because of available time and writing space.

Flipping open the calendar, you see that your daily activities are already listed on its pages. Page after page is filled with all the work you do at home, all the errands you run, all the time you spend teaching and helping your kids, all the volunteer activities you already have committed to do. *Wow!* you say to yourself. *I didn't realize I was so busy! The next time someone tells me I don't work, I'll just flash this baby!* You fish through the tissue again, dying to see what else is in this box. Your hand touches . . .

A Coupon Organizer

Lifting the coupon organizer from the box, you look inside it, and find it already full of coupons—and only for products you actually would buy anyway! *Where on earth did these come from?* you wonder. At the very front of the organizer, you find this note:

Use generously when shopping. Share a few with friends. And remember, take care of your pennies and your dollars will take care of themselves.

Then it hits you! Of course! These are all things you've been reading about in that book, *All Mothers Work*!

Someone went to a lot of trouble for me, you think, digging deeper in the box. Your hand touches another item—something larger. *Oooh, something big.* You pull out a square metal box labeled . . .

Emergency First Aid Kit

You see a note taped to the lid:

Please open before *an emergency event!*

You think about your admonition to the kids earlier, when they were fighting. "I don't want to hear about it unless there's blood involved!" you told them when they tried to drag you into it.

Well, that worked out okay—no emergencies today. I guess I should open this now.

Unlatching the lid, you carefully open the kit. Inside you see only two items: a book labeled *Emergency Manual* and a small acrylic box with something colorful inside.

Must be a book on how to make bandages, you think, *since I don't see any in here.* Curious, you pick up the manual and open it to the first page.

EMERGENCY FIRST AID
FOR AT-HOME MOMS

PART ONE—INTRODUCTION

Welcome to the world of *Emergency First Aid for At-Home Moms*. This kit has two components: the manual you are now reading, and a visual aid (which we will talk about in a minute).

This is a very special manual, having been written specifically for readers of the book *All Mothers Work*. You should be at or about Chapter Thirteen at this point, and have quite possibly mastered the skills set forth in Chapters Eight through Twelve. Thus, you are now qualified to reign as a stay-at-home mom supreme! Now all you have to do is relax and enjoy the ride, right?

Wrong. Sorry. Life is hard and then you die. Those are the rules. And there's another rule that says, "Just when life gets to going the way you want it to, something happens to mess it up." You know the one—it's the same rule that causes the telephone to ring as soon as you sit down to eat dinner. (Don't you just *hate* that rule?)

Yes, crud happens. Hubby loses a job. Or leaves. Or dies. Houses burn down. Cars get wrecked, or need expensive, new thingamajigs. People get sick—and need treatment—even if you don't have enough insurance.

Maybe you would rather not talk about this. To tell you the truth, neither would I. Unfortunately, crud happens whether we talk about it or not. So let's do talk about it, just for a little while. Then we'll get on to happier thoughts.

Deal?

PART TWO—CPR

Let's get right to the heart of the matter. If even one of these cruddy things happens in your life, you need immediate CPR.

Now, I'm not talking about cardiopulmonary resuscitation (although in certain emergencies you might need that also). No, what we're talking about here is Contingency Plan Response. We're talking about creating fallback positions in case some kind of emergency takes over and changes your life.

Are you trained in Contingency Plan Response? Let me ask you another way: Do you have any earthly idea what you would do if, say, your husband dropped dead tomorrow? Have you ever even thought about the possibility?

No matter what is going on in your life today, there is one thing I can absolutely guarantee you: *Things change.* What works for you and your family today will not necessarily work *after* things change. And, *when* things change, you'd better be ready to change with them.

Take me and my family. We enjoy a natural division of labor. Pretty normal stuff, really. I cook most of the meals, and Arnold takes out most of the trash—that sort of thing. If I don't feel like cooking, I simply announce that we're going out, or that everyone is on his own. If the trash piles up, I let him worry about it. It's a good system, and it works for us.

But, if my husband somehow dropped off the face of the planet one day, I'd have to start worrying about the trash (and about a zillion other things), wouldn't I? Oh, I could just continue to let the trash pile up, or pretend it doesn't exist, or hope someone would come along and get rid of it for me—but sooner or later I would have to deal with the trash, and take it out myself.

So won't it save a lot of time if I decide now that if I lose my trash-taker-outer, I'll handle that responsibility myself? Then, if the unthinkable ever does happen, I won't have to worry about what's going to happen with the trash. I'll already know what to do.

I learned about planning for the unexpected from my father, who always has a Plan B. This is a man who—I kid you not—keeps an inflatable raft and an axe in his upstairs bedroom closet, just in case the town floods because of a hurricane or something and he needs to chop his way out through the roof. He's ready for anything!

PART THREE—SHOCK TREATMENT

If you're waiting for me to tell you one very good reason that you should develop a CPR before an emergency comes up, here it is:

*It is very difficult to think when you're in the middle
of a crisis.*

Got that? Chances are, *if* or *when* something terrible happens,
you're going to be in shock. You probably won't even want to
think. Your brain will be sending you messages along the lines
of: "Wake me up when all this is over."

On the other hand, if you've already thought through what
you would do *if*, you won't have to think so hard when the
emergency occurs. You can simply execute your Contingency
Plan Response, and worry about thinking later.

Also, since different kinds of emergencies can and will occur,
you need to develop more than one CPR. For example, I have
one plan for when our budget gets tight (part-time temporary
work) and another for if—heaven forbid—my husband gets
dead (full-time permanent work). Forgive me for being so mor-
bid, but we are talking death and destruction here, aren't we?

What am I doing about those contingency plans now? Well,
to begin with, I signed up with a couple of temporary employment agencies. That way, if I need a job in a hurry, I have
already done the preliminary testing that these agencies require.
And I did it on my time—when I wasn't nervous or upset about
something else. They know me, they know my skills. I'm ready
to hop into a temp job by just picking up the phone and saying,
"Put me to work!"

My contingency plan for my husband dying is a little more
complicated—as well it should be. He has a life insurance policy that would buy me enough time to grieve and adjust to life
without him. I wouldn't want to move—at least not right away.
(Anyway, I'm certain I read somewhere that you're not supposed to move an injured person.) After that, there's always the
kindness of strangers . . .

No, seriously, I figure that by the time I've recovered from
the loss (as much as could be expected), I would be ready to
evaluate the appropriate action to take next. For me, the insurance policy is kind of like my dad's inflatable raft. It's there to
keep me going until the shock wears off, and I can think again.

You may be asking yourself, "What can *I* do to create a contingency plan? And when would I have to do it?"

Such intelligent questions! I'll give you equally intelligent answers. (It's only fair.) You want to do *something*. And you want to do it *now*.

Oh. You want me to be more specific. Okay—if you insist.

PART FOUR—ADVANCED CPR TRAINING

Following are five basic steps you need to complete to develop a successful Contingency Plan Response.

Step One. Think about the unthinkable. This is the hardest step of all, because we don't want to (on purpose) think about the bad things that might happen. I have to admit here that every time Arnold is late coming home, I imagine all sorts of terrible things that might have happened to him. If you do that, too, you're ready to execute step one. If you're out of practice in expecting the worst, take your time. Start with something small, like, "I might get a hangnail." Work your way up slowly to the big, bad, and ugly things.

Step Two. Determine your areas of weakness. Now that you have the unthinkable identified, look at your list again. Go through each item and ask yourself, "Is this something I am ready to handle?" Going back to a previous example, let's say that I have never taken out the trash in my life—that I've never even touched a trashcan. Maybe I'm afraid of trashcans or something. I really *depend* on having someone else around to take out the trash (which isn't too far from the truth).

If I found myself in a situation in which I was the only person available to take out the trash, I would be in trash trouble. I would, therefore, be forced to identify my "trash terror" as an area of weakness.

What are your areas of weakness? Are you afraid to balance the checkbook? (I know that sometimes I am, especially after a trip to my favorite clothing store.) Would you know what to do if your house caught fire? Have you thought about (gasp) where you will bury your dead?

I know this is hard, but try to hang in with me here. You'll feel better later—I promise.

Step Three. Strengthen your areas of weakness. Okay, the hardest part is over. You've probably scared yourself silly by now. The good news is, things can only go uphill from here!

Having identified your areas of weakness, you are ready to work on strengthening those weaknesses. Take my trash (please). While I still have my husband around to take the trash out for me, I could start learning about the process by, say, following him around while he's doing that particular chore. Granted, he would probably tease me about shadowing him like that. But that's okay. I would expect to have to endure *some* hardships to overcome my weakness.

Maybe a weakness you identified was not knowing where your insurance policies are. That's an easy area to strengthen. First, find your policies. (Okay, maybe it's not as easy as I thought.) After you find them, put them in a fireproof safe at home, or in a safe deposit box at the bank. That way, if the house burns down, it won't take your policies with it.

Whatever areas of weakness you identified, use your time *now*, before something terrible happens, to shore up your defenses. You'll be glad you did.

Step Four. Develop your Contingency Plan Response. This step is similar to the step you've just completed, except that it takes things a little further. One step further, as a matter of fact.

In my trash scenario, I identified it as an area of weakness, then I strengthened my weakness by learning the steps involved in taking out the trash. All that remains is developing my trash CPR. I might decide to do this chore (if I must) twice a week— on Monday and Thursday mornings. I can write this procedure down and file it away for future reference.

Let's look at those insurance policies again. After you've found them and put them in a safe place, you might develop a CPR in which you would write down the steps necessary to file a claim. Call your agent and ask him or her to tell you the correct procedure. Write down all the details and telephone numbers you will need, then put that list with your policies.

That way you won't have to read a bunch of fine print trying to find the information when you're upset.

Step Five. Where appropriate, start CPR before an emergency. I have good news for you. You don't have to wait until an emergency happens to put your Contingency Plan Response into action. There are many things you can do—right now—that would help you prepare in advance for a possible emergency.

If, for example, you think you would go back to school if your husband died, why not go back to school now? You could take one course at a time if you wanted to. The main point is, you would be well on your way with your plan if and when the emergency happened.

You might choose to do volunteer work related to your old job, to keep up with what's going on in that area. Or maybe you would want to start some kind of in-home business to build a nest egg of savings to fall back on in case of financial emergencies.

The main point, which I'm sure you've realized by now, is *be prepared*! Then relax. What will be, will be.

PART FIVE—THE VISUAL AID

Go ahead and pick up the acrylic box you found next to this manual. Look inside it. You will see a carefully preserved butterfly. (Okay, so there really isn't a box, but a girl can imagine can't she?)

The butterfly is here to remind us that things change, because the butterfly itself was once a caterpillar. It was required to make some pretty major changes in its life, with spectacular results! When we are challenged with having to change, our results can be just as spectacular. Change, even if prompted by negative circumstances, doesn't always have to be negative.

That's all. Get those contingency plans going, and have a nice day.

Closing the manual, you reach over and pick up the acrylic box, and admire the beautiful butterfly mounted inside. You look at all the items on the floor around you.

Someone did go to a lot of trouble for me, you think. Then you smile.

Because you know this care package is a gift you give yourself.

CHAPTER 14

HOW TO BE THE RICHEST MOM IN TOWN

(. . .whether or not you actually have any money)

If we learn how to give ourselves, to forgive others, and to live with thanksgiving, we need not seek happiness—it will seek us.
                    —JOSEPH FORT NEWTON, 1950

THE SEARCH FOR CONTENTMENT

What would it take for you to feel happy and content with your life?

Come on, tell the truth. Money? Power? A big house? Healthy kids? (Or maybe kids who have grown up and moved out!)

I carry around in my head a little list of things I want. Things that will make me happy. My own office instead of a computer in the corner of the bedroom—that desire looms large in my mind these days. Enough money to get even with the creditors. And please—self-cleaning toilets.

There used to be other things on my list. Items that I have slowly acquired through the years. There's my in-home cross-country ski machine (extremely low mileage—available at a deep discount). I always knew if I just had one of those machines I would exercise every day and lose ten pounds in six weeks and then I would be content. I figured the toilets would stay clean on their own out of respect for my newly discovered peace of mind.

Naturally, it didn't work that way. The cross-country ski machine turned into a dusty clothing rack and the toilets didn't respond one way or the other. I discovered that exercise equipment doesn't make me happy—it makes me feel guilty because I'm not using it. Likewise, a new car doesn't make me happy. Well, okay, maybe it did for a while . . . until it wasn't new anymore. Even going to my favorite clothing store doesn't make me happy. Well dressed and broke, maybe. But happy? Not really.

So how do we find happiness? What do you think will make you happy? And remember, tell the truth.

THE TRUTH SHALL MAKE YOU FREE

When I was about eighteen, my mother came home from running errands one day, all excited about something she had seen on the way home.

"I saw this really great billboard," she said as she came through the door. "It said . . . well, I don't remember exactly what it said. But it meant . . ." She paused to think for a minute. "Well, I can't remember exactly what it meant, either . . . but it was really memorable!"

We laughed. Mom was so enthusiastic about this billboard, I had to go see it for myself. Fortunately, she *did* remember its location, even if she didn't remember anything else about it! I hopped into the car and drove down the road, and sure enough, there it was, bigger than life:

THE TRUTH SHALL MAKE YOU FREE!
But First, It Will Make You Miserable

Mom was right. It really was memorable! I drove home immediately and told her what it said, so that she could remember it, too. We still laugh about that day.

The truth shall make you free, but first it will make you miserable. How true. When I made the decision to be a stay-at-home mom, I had to face the truth about what my "job behavior" was doing to my son. And facing that truth did make me miserable, because I had to admit that I had not been giving my son what he *really* needed. I had to take responsibility for the fallout of my choice to be so totally focused on my job to the exclusion of my family.

Coming home didn't solve every problem I have with being a parent, but it helped—a lot! And I do feel free—free from always being in a hurry, free from the stress of an outside job, free from the idea that I have to make a lot of money to be worthy of breathing. My wardrobe isn't what it used to be, but all in all, it was a fair trade.

To be content, and free, we have to go through that "miserable" part. And the tricky thing is, it's an ongoing process. We have to keep examining our lives and our choices—checking ourselves to see if we're on track with what's really important.

But finding that truth, and facing it, isn't always easy. I'm not sure it ever is. Fortunately, I have a little something here that may help.

THE ROCKING CHAIR TEST

When I need to see the truth in my life, I give myself the rocking chair test. Now, don't be alarmed. You don't actually need a rocking chair to administer the test. It's very easy to do—safe and harmless. First, I close my eyes. Then I imagine that I'm sitting in a rocking chair and that I'm really, really old (that part gets easier every day)—so old that all my friends have died. I'm all alone. Sitting in my rocking chair. All I have left are my memories.

Next, I try to imagine what my memories are. Am I wishing

I had spent more time on my accounting career? Or am I glad I made the choice to be home with my son while that choice was still open to me? It seems like so long ago. He was young for such a very short time. Just an instant. Now he's grown and has a family of his own. He comes to see me when he can, but it's hard for him with his busy schedule. I'm glad I have those memories of taking him to school, listening to him afterward when he'd had a hard day. I'm glad I had to cart him all over creation until he learned to drive. I'm glad I didn't miss my chance to be with him. It's funny, but looking back, it doesn't seem to matter a bit that we didn't have cable TV. Or that I quit having my fingernails painted by strangers. All those things I worried about giving up—they don't seem to matter at all. I think of our little house with too few rooms and too many pets. And I smile. I am content.

The rocking chair test is how I keep in touch with the choices I'm making today. It's a way to look at those choices from a different perspective—to "try on" how those choices feel by looking at them as if they had already happened. I have a big fear of getting to that rocking chair time of my life and looking back with regret. I do not want to say to myself, "I wish I'd done this," or "I wish I hadn't done that."

Mary, a mom in Ohio who journeyed home from the workplace, understands the concept of the rocking chair test: "I doubt very much whether I will remember any of the endless business meetings or deadlines from years past, but I will remember the delicious feeling of extra snuggles with a toddler, or being there with enough energy to hold my husband after his tough day outside our warm house."

The rocking chair test also helps me to stretch my boundaries. I gave myself the test when I got the offer to write this book. I'd never written a book before and it was a very big and scary commitment. Could I do it? I wasn't sure. I tried to imagine myself, rocking away, saying, "Yes, I had a chance, once, to write a book, but I didn't do it because it was too scary." Thinking about saying that to myself didn't feel very good. I realized it would be easier to give myself permission to go for my dream of writing than to try to forgive myself later for not even trying. Taking the rocking chair test gave me the courage to take on something new—to say, "Yes, I'll do it."

It's a good idea to take the rocking chair test even when you're not contemplating major life decisions. Use it as a spot check for what you're doing with your life today. Just close your eyes and imagine yourself fifty years down the road (with luck you'll still be alive), remembering the life you're living right now. Does it feel good to remember your life? Are you content with the choices you're making? Do you have any regrets, any unfulfilled dreams? Are your children still speaking to you?

And speaking of the children, you can even incorporate them into the test. Imagine, for a moment, that you are your child—grown up. I understand that this might take a little doing. I mean, sometimes it's hard to understand what they're thinking! But try anyway. Try to put yourself in your child's shoes and imagine what kind of childhood you will remember twenty or thirty years from now. What you see, looking back at today through your child's eyes, may surprise you.

If it's truth you're looking for, the rocking chair test is a good way to find it. If what you find makes you miserable, don't worry. There's still hope for you to get to where you want to be.

THE ROAD TO RICHES

I want to be the richest mom in town. In many ways, I already am, because I have many treasures. One treasure is the love of my husband. Another is a happy, healthy child who I pray has the confidence to become everything he was meant to be. I treasure my health, because the better I feel, the more stuff I can get done (and I have a lot of stuff to do). And I treasure my friends, because I like having people to do some of that stuff with.

Do you want to be rich? Do you want me tell you how to be rich?

Well, I can't.

That's the point, isn't it? The secret to being the richest mom in town is to take an honest look at your life, and then make the choices for your life that work for you. For me, being rich means being home, setting my own schedule and being available to do things with my son after school. It means cooking dinner for my family, and having my husband clean the kitchen. Because my life works for me, it is rich and rewarding *to me*. Now, if I could just find those self-cleaning toilets . . .

I'm sure you've noticed that I have carefully avoided saying that being rich has anything to do with having a lot of money. I guess that makes me a romantic. I love watching those old movies like *Penny Serenade,* about people who find love and happiness without any money and through heartbreaking tragedy in a two-room apartment.

As appealing as those old movies are, sometimes I think about real people I've read about who have lived through tragedies. You know, people who survive airplane crashes or escape from burning houses in the nick of time. So many of them talk about discovering what's really important to them, and it isn't money.

So I figure, why wait for a tragedy? If I can make my life work for me and my family—whether or not we have a lot of money—then I can be content. And if I can be content with my life, I'll have the kind of riches no one can ever take away.

And so can you.

Ode to Joy

Joy turned the page of the photo album she held in her lap as she sat nestled in her favorite rocker. A soft breeze came through the open window, cooling her face and bringing with it the aroma of the honeysuckle vine on the nearby trellis. When she came to the picture of Herby at his twelfth birthday party, she smiled. The tiny lines that had begun to form around her eyes crinkled together.

He'll be going away soon, she thought, her smile fading. Hannah was already out on her own, studying pre-law halfway across the country. And Herby—well, *if* he managed to graduate from high school, he had plans of his own making. That boy had always had more energy than he needed! He couldn't wait to get started with his life— and was already talking about getting a job and moving in with a friend.

Joy shook her head and turned another page. All her memories of her children's growing-up years were tucked into this album. Lately, she found herself looking through it every time she walked near the coffee table.

"You're living in the past again, aren't you?" Dan asked her once. He had come into the room and found her sitting there with the album spread open before her.

"I'm just trying to remember what you looked like with hair," she answered with a mischievous grin.

But today, she was alone in the house. She turned the album pages quietly while reflecting on all the choices she had made in her life. It hadn't been easy for them. Money had always been a problem. No matter how much money there was, it never seemed to be quite enough. But somehow, the struggles they had gone through didn't show up in the pictures in front of her.

There were hints, of course, like the vacation photos over the years that all had the same old station wagon in the background. And the photographic evidence in the album revealed that Joy had worn the same outfit three Thanksgivings in a row. Then there was the year they hadn't taken any pictures—the year she and Dan had been fighting. The memories were there, in part because the pictures weren't.

She lingered for a moment over Hannah's prom picture, her fingers touching the image of the dress that Hannah had worked so hard to buy. Joy's smile returned. With it came a sudden, intense feeling of pride in her two children.

"I wouldn't change a thing," she said softly to herself.

The front door open with a rush of sudden activity. "Mom!" Herby called out. "Mom, where are you?"

Joy closed the album and looked over her shoulder. "I'm in the living room, son."

Herby ran into the room, out of breath. "Mom! I got that job at the lumberyard!" His words tumbled out as if he couldn't say them fast enough. "As soon as school's out, I'll be able to get that apartment with Nick. Isn't it great?"

Joy looked at her son. She knew this was one of those moments when she had to say the right thing, even though the only thought going through her mind was, *My baby— he's leaving!* Laying the album aside, she stood up.

I'm not going to get any sleep tonight, she thought, and walked over to congratulate her son.

The Bottom Line

I'll be honest with you. I started this book more or less as a reflex in defense of mothers who choose to stay home. I was tired of the "Do you work?" question and skeptical that all those who said they "had" to work really had no choices.

From this little seed of discontent grew a new understanding of us mothers—every last one of us. (Yes, I know I said this book wasn't for everyone, but it really is. So sue me.)

We're all just doing the best we can with what we have. I am. You are. Your mother-in-law is.

And we're allowed to change, and to learn, and to grow.

And to make choices.

The truth is, we each have something unique to offer to our world and to the people around us. Part of my offering has been this book. But it was also endless hours of preparing financial statements at one point in my life and running after-school car pools for my son at another.

You are a fascinating, talented, multifaceted individual! I know you are, because I was given a gift from each woman who shared her life with me as I prepared these pages. Each taught me something I didn't know, gave me something I didn't have before. If you and I had an opportunity to sit down over a cup of coffee, I know the same would hold true of you. And I would listen with fascination for what I could learn from you.

The bottom line is, what's really important is not which choice you make, but that you make choices that make sense for you. Many will argue that the best choice for the kids is to have mom at home, and I would have to agree with them. But even if that's the ideal, staying home isn't a viable option for everyone.

So you have to choose your life based on what's going to work for you. You know yourself best, after all. You know your own dreams and desires, your restrictions and limitations. When you're resting in that rocking chair toward the end of your life, you know what kind of life you want to look back on and remember.

Now is the time to make that life for yourself. Are you unhappy? Make a change! Do you have dreams of a different kind of life? Go for it! Do you have a hidden talent you've been afraid to let show? Give yourself permission to try!

I hope you recognize how truly special you are, and how very capable you are of making good decisions for your life. No apologies. Whatever you choose, as long as it works for you (*and it's legal!*), I'm on your side.

I hope we got that straight!

APPENDIX

P.S. My book runneth over

For those of you who want to examine the possibilities of making money with a home-based business, I recommend you access the many excellent resources available at your local bookstore or library. I found the following books particularly helpful:

Working From Home—Everything You Need to Know About Living and Working Under the Same Roof, by Paul and Sarah Edwards, Tarcher/Putnam, 1994.

The Best Home Businesses for the '90s, by Paul and Sarah Edwards, Tarcher/Putnam, 1991.

101 Best Home-Based Businesses for Women, by Priscilla Y. Huff, Prima, 1995.

In the meantime, here's a partial list of home-based business possibilities to whet your appetite:

IF YOU WANT TO STAY CLOSE TO HOME:

Academic tutor
Artist
Arts and crafts
Auto detailing
Bookkeeper
Business plan writer
Button-making business
Cake decorating
Calligraphy
Chocolate candy maker
Clipping service
Computer programmer
Contract abstractor
Copywriter
Custom photo albums
Data entry
Desktop publisher
Directory publication service
Facialist
Fitness trainer
Freelance writer
Furniture refinisher
Gift wrapping service
Greeting card verse writer
Grower of specialty foods
Hair stylist
Home day care provider
Income tax preparer
Indexer
Information search and retrieval service
Mail order business

Mailing list service
Manicurist
Medical billing service
Medical transcription service
Newsletter editor/publisher
Outside sales travel agent
Paralegal
Personalized children's books
Piano teacher
Picture framing business
Potpourri maker
Proofreader/copyeditor
Résumé writer/preparer
Seamstress
Stock market technical researcher
Tape duplication service
Technical writer
Telemarketer
Telephone answering service
Translator
Typing service

IF YOU LIKE GETTING OUT OF THE HOUSE:

Balloon business
Caterer
Cleaning service
Computer consultant
Computer service and repair
Corporate trainer
Cosmetic sales and consultant
Health product sales
Home appraiser
Home childproofing service
Home inspector
Home inventory service

House number painting
Housesitting service
Image consultant
Interior designer
Laundry service
Management consultant
Party planner
Pet watching service
Professional organizer
Professional practice consultant
Public relations specialist
Publicist
Real estate consultant
Shopping and errand service
Singing telegram service
Videographer
Wedding makeup artist
Wedding planner
Window treatment consultant